I CAN PLAY IT

First edition for the United States, its territories and dependencies and Canada published in 2015 by Barron's Educational Series, Inc.

All inquiries should be addressed to:
Barron's Educational Series, Inc.
250 Wireless Boulevard
Hauppauge, New York 11788
www.barronseduc.com

ISBN: 978-1-4380-0707-6

Library of Congress Catalog Card No.: 2015936754

Conceived and produced by
Elwin Street Productions
3 Percy Street
London W1T 1DE
United Kingdom
www.elwinstreet.com

Illustrator: Isabel Alberdi

Printed and bound in China

9 8 7 6 5 4 3 2 1

I CAN PLAY IT

**Music games and activities
to help your child learn**

Patricia Shehan Campbell

Montessori consultant: Maja Pitamic
Music education consultant: Christopher Roberts

Bradford WG Public Library
425 Holland St. W.
Bradford, ON L3Z 0J2

Contents

Chapter 4 MUSIC AT HOME `80`

Chapter 5 OUTDOOR MUSIC `112`

RESOURCES `138`

Foreword by Maja Pitamic

From the beginning of civilization, humankind has found expression through the arts in disciplines that include drawing, painting, poetry, stories, and music. Of these disciplines, music—in all forms—is the most fundamental, an innate presence within every one of us. It is natural for us to express ourselves vocally. Even when a baby is born, the first thing he or she will do is cry to make his or her presence known in the world.

An early-twentieth-century leading revolutionary educationalist, Maria Montessori, recognized the importance of the development of the auditory sense alongside the other four senses from an early age and acknowledged the roles each sense played in child development. She observed that, from birth to about six or seven years of age, children entered what she described as "sensitive periods"—times of heightened sensitivity within their five senses. She called the senses a child's natural learning tools and created a classroom environment in which sensitive periods were responded to through auditory activities.

The activities in *I Can Play It* recognize the importance of the senses in child development and seek to engage children in music using multisensory approaches. In doing so, the activities draw significantly on the pedagogies of Carl Orff, Zoltán Kodály, and Émile Jacques-Dalcroze, who, like Montessori, recognized a child's natural abilities for rhythm, movement, and song.

Whenever I have been involved with children's music making, the engagement of the child has been total and absolute. I hope that you will be similarly engaged with your child when you explore the activities in this book together, instilling a lasting love of music as you do so.

Pathways of musical development

All young children are singers, players, dancers, listeners, and creators of music. They are musical from birth and, by the time they emerge from toddlerhood, are enriched with a multitude of musical experiences. They enjoy making music alone, together, within families, and among friends. And just as they are able to express themselves in language, young children are equally capable of expressing themselves through music.

I Can Play It is filled with ideas for introducing a wide range of musical practices to young children between the ages of three and five. The book encourages you to enter into the world of your child with a host of musical games. The activities are grounded in established developmental practices yet require no specialized knowledge or equipment.

Musical ways, means, and outcomes

The activities in this book invite you to help your child develop the capacity to listen, touch, and feel music through song, play, and movement. Your child's listening skills will be enhanced from the moment you start and will continue to develop as you explore the activities further.

Through practicing these activities, your child will develop strong cognitive (mental), kinesthetic (movement), and social-emotional skills through music that is everywhere "in the air" and in the environment in which you both live.

In the cognitive sense, your child will gain a better understanding of all aspects of music. When children sort through ways of making sounds, they also learn to discriminate between a wide diversity of tone colors. Meanwhile, the invention of rhymes and short verses affirms and enriches a growing storage of language.

Kinesthetically, every pulse-making activity, every move and groove, and every gesture in response to high-low or fast-slow is an indication that there is a flow between what a child hears and what the body feels and expresses.

A child's social-emotional development is assured through shared performances and explorations; activities that require two or more to sing, play, or dance together; and experiences that call for parent-child dialogue in music and about music.

Musical practices

Orff, Kodály, and Dalcroze are widely known practices when it comes to exploring music with young children. Each honors a child's interests and needs and offers playful experiences with music that lead to growth of skills in performing, listening, and creating. They arise from the work of European-based composers, performers, and pedagogues from the first half of the twentieth century: Carl Orff (1895–1982) of Germany, Zoltán Kodály (1882–1967) of Hungary, and Émile Jacques-Dalcroze (1865–1950) of Switzerland.

These musicians acknowledged the importance of learning by listening, and by observation and imitation, and they sought to celebrate the possibilities for exploration and improvisation as important child-appropriate avenues of understanding. They saw the importance to children of rhythm, communally made music, and movement as inherent in music. They could not have known the extent to which their work would later be supported by neuroscientific research, nor how their recommendations would be embraced by parents and teachers for years to come.

■ The Orff approach extols the natural behaviors of childhood as the starting place for learning. Teaching is closely linked to the young child's world of fantasy and play—of games, songs, and speech chants. The critical characteristic is a child's exploratory experiences with music, movement, and speech (and sometimes all three together and overlapping). Four stages of the Orff process unfold over time: imitation, preliminary exploration, literacy (that is, reading notation), and creative improvisation on a melody or rhythm.

■ The Kodály approach places an emphasis on singing and careful and attentive listening and asserts that music is the right of all children. This right comes with responsibility by parents and other adults to draw out the music that is there within each child's capacity, and to provide opportunities to discover folk and art music at its finest.

Since all children have singing voices and dancing bodies, these activities are recommended from the earliest ages—and long before any formal training should commence for learning to read and write music and to play instruments.

■ The Dalcroze tradition is associated with a unique type of movement known as eurhythmics (or "good rhythm") that results from careful and concentrated listening to music's features.

The rhythm of a song, the rise-and-fall of a melody, and the choppy or smooth quality of a musical selection can set a child to physically express in her body what she hears. The ear-body-brain link of Dalcroze exercises unfolds a process that frontloads listening and provides occasions for feeling it through physical movement, so that musical understanding and skills can be more deeply known.

This book takes the best of Orff, Kodály, and Dalcroze practices and applies it to the musical experiences that you and your child can share.

How to use this book

This book provides musical experiences for the sake of the music itself and for the outcomes that emerge through experiences. The developmental levels of young children are very much in mind, as are their shared musical meanings, interests, and needs. The activities require little expertise, the preparations are minimal, and the few materials used are standard household items or other easily available materials. The activities are designed to interest and amuse your child, and both of you will benefit from them.

■ All of the activities are gender neutral and are suitable for both boys and girls. For the sake of variety, the use of "she" and "he" alternates within the chapters.

■ Check your environment. Make sure that you and your child can do the activity in comfort and safety, both in the home and in public spaces.

■ Clear an area for singing, dancing, and playing that can serve as a rehearsal and performance space. Keep it clear, so that your child can return to it if he wishes.

■ Prepare an activity in advance, assembling materials and clearing a space if necessary.

■ Make sure your child can see and hear the activity clearly, especially when playing instruments or other sound sources.

■ Sit your child to the left of you (to your right if you are right-handed), and work with your right hand (your left, if your child is left-handed) for consistency.

■ Review the steps of each activity to ensure that all is in order and ready to go. Try them out in advance as practice for smooth flow from one step to the next. Be clear in your own mind what the aim of the activity is.

■ Work through activities with numbered steps in the suggested sequence of steps, so as to appeal to the sense of logic and order.

- With activities with no sequence (that is, without step numbers), you can pick and choose to suit your child.

- Make good use of eye contact with your child, especially when activities involve musical games.

- Confirm that the volume of any music you play is pleasing to your child—neither too loud nor too soft—and adjust as necessary.

- Maintain a flow in the song, rhythm, chant, or other experience, without too many starts and stops that could distract and disinterest your child.

- Accept that your child may need more time; modeling; or repetition of a sound, idea, or pattern. Allow him to practice a step as many times as he wishes. A child learns through repetition.

- Abandon an activity that may appear confusing, frustrating, or uninteresting to your child. The activity may feel right and ready at another point in time.

- Be positive and encouraging of your child's participation, yet realistic in that some musical experiences may take time to ease into.

- Model good listening behavior, and expect it from your child.

- Require respect for musical instruments, recordings, and materials for each activity. If your child abuses any of the materials, remove the activity immediately. He will understand his behavior was unacceptable. Resume the activity at a later date.

- Remember that these are "we" activities, and that your child can participate in all segments—including setup and cleanup.

Learning together

- If you don't know the answer to a question, say that you don't know and see if you can find out the answer together.

- While a structured approach is needed, allow yourself to be flexible and don't worry if things don't always go as planned.

Frequently asked questions

How old should my child be before she is presented with an activity?

■ These activities are intended for children aged three to five years. Many of them are "sliding ventures," which means they can be successfully experienced by children across the age span. Some may be performed better by older rather than younger children within the spectrum, while others will hold the attention of younger children better than older children. Children in this age range will enjoy the activities but will also achieve a sense of accomplishment.

Is there an order of activities to follow?

■ The activities are organized in such a way that they progress from the simpler concepts to the more complex within each chapter. The activities do not have to be practiced one after the other, but younger children may find the more complex concepts easier if they are already familiar with the simpler ones.

What if I can't sing?

■ If you can speak, you can sing—all but about four percent of humanity can sing.

You may sing softly, or within a limited range of pitches, or a little out of tune. You may not have the confidence to sing in front of others. But you can sing, and your child will appreciate your singing. You can encourage your child to sing by singing— and also by listening and responding in a positive manner.

What if I don't play a musical instrument?

■ Most of the activities in the book do not involve playing a musical instrument. There are various activities involving the playing of "found sounds"—local objects from kitchens and bedrooms, from the yard, or from nature. Some activities involve the simple construction of pretend instruments that look, but may not sound, like real instruments.

What if I can't dance?

■ To dance is human! Everyone can move, as it is part of our human anatomy to wave our hands, nod our heads, lift our shoulders, wiggle our hips, and shift our weight from one foot to the other. When the music starts, step to it, clap to it, sway from side to side to it: That's the beginning of the dance we may wish to do. Watch your child move naturally to music, and join in. While it's true that some folks have fancy moves that they have learned through observation, imitation, and practice, you can dance in ways that are simple and connected to the musical beat, tempo, and character.

What if my child makes a mistake?

■ The activities are meant to invite children and parents into an experience. There is no need to judge the quality of the participation, or to dwell on a mistake (in speaking a poem or in tapping a rhythm, for example). Instead, the activities are aimed at providing pathways for you and your child to experience, explore, and experiment with music.

When is the best time in the day to engage in music?

■ Some of the musical activities are destined for particular times of day, such as the lullabies for bedtime or the wake-up music in the morning. Most of the activities are "timeless," that is, to be experienced at any time. Young children may be able to concentrate best in the mornings, after a good night's sleep, or following a resting period (such as a nap), so consider these times for maximal impact on learning. But truly, music can happen through the day, and in many locations.

What if my child does not seem to respond to the activity?

■ Not every child is ready for every experience that a parent would like to show and share. If your child is not interested in an activity, there is no reason to persist. Rather, plan for another time, and ask yourself whether there were circumstances that caused disinterest: the wrong time of day or a lackluster, uncertain, or confusing presentation.

Our very own music

Claps and taps, shouts and whispers

What better place to discover the making of music than by exploring our very own bodies for potential? Children explore their vocal capacities from an early age and make all sorts of percussion sounds using their hands, fingers, and feet. This chapter provides you with activities to encourage your child to make her very own music. She will thrill at the range of possibilities for playing with melody, rhythm, tone color (timbre), and form—especially when she joins with you in making the music happen.

Children own the music that is very near to them. It emanates from them and them alone—their singing voices and their claps, taps, snaps, and stamps. What unfolds from practicing the activities in this chapter is the recognition that you and your child can become primary sources of musical sound. The activities selected feature such musical concepts as high and low, long and short, and loud and soft as revealed through Orff-oriented speech rhythms, the vocal play and singing practices pioneered by Kodály, and Dalcroze-inspired kinesthetic movement to music.

A number of the activities in this section may require some props—that is, readily available materials such as cups, a scarf, and a ball—but most of the music can be performed simply enough by you and your child. Help your child to listen to, and explore, the musical possibilities that live within all of us, or that can be achieved with minimal effort using our hands and feet. This is the music that we make with our very own selves!

Tummy tapping

Our tummies! That all-important body part, smack in the center of our beings, plays an important role in digesting the food that we eat. For singers, muscles in the stomach are important for developing good vocal technique. And for toddlers, tummies are just plain fun! Marching around with stomachs stuck out is an age-specific thing to do, and young children all the way up to school age find it uproariously entertaining.

1 Start by exploring your tummy as a drum! With your child watching, take your fingers and drum them on your own stomach. Try tapping different areas, using just your fingers or your whole hand, to see how the sound changes. What happens to the sound when you use a wooden spoon?

You will need

• Basic kitchen utensils

Tummy tapping *continued*

2 Encourage your child to copy you. You can try drumming each other's tummies, too, and prepare yourself for laughter—sometimes even before the tapping actually occurs!

3 Think about the different foods your child ate at his last meal and make a list. Make a non-rhyming short poem out of the different foods—for example, "Hamburger, green beans, bananas, and ice cream." Repeat it over and over again with your child.

Tip Overenthusiastic children may be tempted to tummy tap too hard. Remind your child to be gentle, particularly when tapping someone else's stomach. Demonstrate an appropriate pressure to use.

4 Once your child has the poem memorized and can say it repeatedly, add some tummy taps on the beat. Each of you can play out the beat using fingers to start with. Then find a variety of different-sized spoons—metal or wood—from the kitchen, and use those to tap the beat.

5 Work on your child's musical memory. Try making up a short poem about something your child likes to eat and personalize it by adding his name. We have used a poem about ice cream (see below), but you could use candy, fruit, vegetables, or whatever you choose.

6 Say the poem and name one kind of ice cream— "vanilla." Repeat the poem, adding a different kind of ice cream, but keeping the first one—"chocolate, vanilla." Encourage your child to join in. Follow the pattern, adding one more type of ice cream each time— "mint chocolate chip, chocolate, vanilla." How many can your child list before losing track?

Other activities to try

When memorizing a poem, to make it more interesting, try adding some changes in volume, starting with a soft voice and growing louder.

Many babies have tummy time, where they lay on their stomachs in order to develop certain motor skills. For a challenge, see if your child can sing at the same time.

Memory Poem

Here is our made-up poem for working on musical memory:

Jean, Jean, dressed in green
Went upstairs to eat ice cream
What kind of ice cream did
she eat?

Hands together

Our hands help us to accomplish so many things, from carrying heavy boxes to scratching an itch. Hands also allow us to make music: Big-kid instrumental players use their hands to strum guitars, play piano keys, and pat drums. By themselves, too, hands can make a surprisingly varied range of musical sounds.

Tip   Do not feel concerned if your child cannot perform the beat accurately. Clapping the beat at the correct time is a developmental skill that often does not occur until late preschool or early elementary school.

1 Leading by demonstration, show your child how to experiment with clapping in different ways. Clap with your fingers pressed tightly together, then with fingers spread apart. Clap so that the fingers of the right hand clap the left palm, then the left fingers clap the right palm. Try a palms-only clap, then a fingers-only clap. Slow down the speed, so that the hands move toward each other slowly. The possibilities are endless.

2 Without any music, start a slow clap and encourage your child to clap in time with you. Gradually make the claps faster and faster. See how long you and your child can keep the claps happening at the same time. Try reversing the order, starting with a faster clap and slowing down (this will be much harder!).

3 Choose a favorite song—either a recorded tune or one that you and your child like to sing. Sit with your child on your lap and place your hands on the backs of her hands. Clap along with the beat of the song, guiding your child's clapping. After practicing a while—and if your child seems ready—see if she can clap the beat without your assistance.

Another activity to try

If you know hand-clapping games from your own childhood, teach them to your child. Children younger than five or six will likely find the coordination involved in these games difficult to master, but they will still enjoy the experience of clapping with you!

Pats and claps

Music is filled with opportunities to join in through rhythmicking—that is, sounding the rhythms—through body percussion. Patting and clapping are popular means of rhythmicking through body percussion, and everyone can join in by patting hands to their laps and by clapping alone or as part of a group. This activity allows for both independent and group participation with music of all kinds.

Tip

The ability to perform patterns of different movements develops over time, so do not be concerned if your child does not achieve the skills immediately. It is most important that you and your child have fun together.

1 Begin by singing a favorite song with your child, and pat your lap along with the beat of the song. Encourage your child to copy you. Sing the song again, this time clapping the beat of the song. Which does your child like better?

2 Make up a short pattern of claps and pats—for example, one pat followed by two claps. Invite your child to echo the pattern. Once practiced a couple times, repeat the process, but with a different pattern (say, two pats and two claps). Gradually increase the difficulty, with pats and claps alternating, or extending the pattern to a combination of five or six movements.

3 Take one of the easier patterns from Step 2—for example, two pats followed by two claps. Working together with your child, see how many times you can repeat the pattern without a mistake. Once your child performs the pattern five times in a row without fail, lengthen the exercise (for example, three pats and four claps) just for the challenge!

4 What else can you find to pat? Create another pattern, but include other places to pat, such as your head, shoulders, or the floor. Start with two places—patting your head and lap, for example—and then add a third.

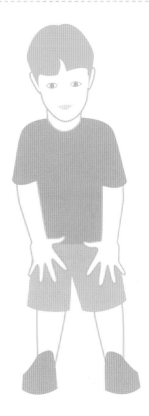

Stepping up

Children typically creep and crawl before they take their first steps. Frequently, they even try to run before gaining full control of a well-balanced walking style. Most become skilled and steady walkers by the age of three. In the next several years, a child will develop her own walking rhythm and develop the muscular coordination to walk in various styles. She'll hop and jump, and soon gallop and skip. This activity provides an opportunity for your child to feel a walking rhythm, first by stepping it, and then by transferring it to handheld blocks and cups.

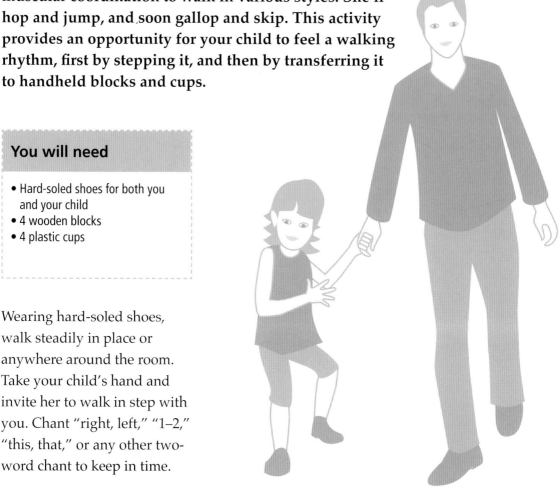

You will need

- Hard-soled shoes for both you and your child
- 4 wooden blocks
- 4 plastic cups

1 Wearing hard-soled shoes, walk steadily in place or anywhere around the room. Take your child's hand and invite her to walk in step with you. Chant "right, left," "1–2," "this, that," or any other two-word chant to keep in time.

2 Play a favorite recording, or find some music on the radio or Internet. Walk to the music with your child, still chanting words such as "right, left," "1–2," or "this, that."

3 Sit down on the floor. Take two wooden blocks—one in each hand— and show your child how to walk them across the floor. Encourage her to copy you with her own wooden blocks. While chanting "1–2," walk them forward and back again, to one side and then the other. As your child repeats the exercise, tell her to listen to the sounds the blocks make on the floor surface.

4 Still sitting on the floor, exchange the wooden blocks for plastic cups and walk them across the floor, chanting "1–2." Point out the different sounds made by blocks and cups.

5 Standing again, try walking steadily with your child, with or without music. This time, count "1–2–3–4," while stepping strongly on *1*.

6 To vary the activity, walk steadily with and without music, counting "1–2–3–4," while stepping strongly on *1* and *3*, and later on *2* and *4*.

> **Tip** The stepping exercises are best performed on uncarpeted floors, which will make the best sounds. Kitchen floors—with ceramic tiles, linoleum, or wooden floorboards—are often the most suitable.

Rise and fall

It is the rising and falling of notes that gives us melodies—small pockets of sound joined together to create memorable tunes. Highs and lows can be found throughout our daily lives as well. This activity encourages your child to explore vocal versions of higher and lower sounds informally and without trying to be in tune. Simply playing with contour can be a joyful way to experience this essential aspect of music. More structured melody making can be found in Chapter 3.

You will need

- Soft ball
- Paper and pencil
- Hand puppet

1 Take a soft ball, throw it up in the air, and, with your child, watch it fall to the floor. Tell him that, just as a ball can go up and then down, one's voice can do the same. Take turns at throwing the ball into the air. Show your child how to mirror the arc of the ball using your voice like a siren and saying "ooOOOOoo."

2 Take your child's hand, and climb into a pretend elevator. Crouch down, saying "first floor" in a low voice. Ride the elevator to different floors, moving your body higher or lower as the floors change. At each floor, stop and say the name of the floor in a higher or lower voice. Ask your child to copy your movements and listen to the voices you use. After several floor changes, continue with the movements and invite your child to call out the floor level in a high, medium, or low voice instead.

3 Ask your child to name a favorite place that you both go to. Draw a picture with your home to one side and your child's favorite place to the other. Draw a squiggly line between the two of them. With you going first, take turns tracing the line with a finger while using your voice to follow the highs and lows of the line: "ooOOOoooOOOoooOOOoo."

Other activities to try

Watch the world around you for places where objects move higher and lower, and demonstrate their patterns using your voice for example, leaves falling from trees or a football being kicked up in the air.

Explore the exercise further using Worksheet 1.

Tip Don't worry if the arc of your child's voice does not exactly mirror the picture or movement that he is following. That is a challenging skill!

Long and short

Some of the beauty found in music is the way in which it moves in long and short sounds. Even in a simple melody, each sound can be compared to the next as either faster, slower, or the very same. Speech, too, contains long and short sounds depending on how individual words are formed. Offer your child a chance to listen and respond to long and short sounds and to create long and short phrases using sticks and a rubber band.

You will need

- Favorite recording
- Favorite poem
- Pair of wooden sticks
- Rubber band

1 Facing your child, play a favorite recording and use your hands and arms to depict the length of the sounds. Flick your fingers and wrists quickly for short sounds. Stretch and wave your arms widely for long sounds. Invite your child to copy you.

2 With the music turned off, try out other long and short sounds. You make the sounds first and then ask your child to copy you. Hum a single tone as long as a deep breath will allow, "h-u-u-u-u-m-m-m-m." Hum short, single-tone sounds: "hmm, hmm, hmm, hmm," breathing quickly between each sound.

3 Recite a favorite poem. We have selected "Room on the Broom" by Julia Donaldson (see right), but you might choose any poem. Read slowly and note those words and syllables that seem to fly by, while others take their time. In our poem compare, for example, "cat" and "spat" to "wailed" and "grinned."

4 Taking a pair of wooden sticks, begin to click the sticks together or on a tabletop as you recite the short sounds in the poem. Say and play the phrases multiple times, noting how short the stick-clicking sounds are.

5 Now invite your child to experiment with the idea of long sounds. Show her how to stretch a rubber band while speaking the longer and slower words of the poem. Meanwhile, you can continue to click sticks on the short sounds.

Poem activity

Room on the Broom

*The witch had a cat
and a very tall hat,
And long ginger hair
which she wore in a plait.*

*How the cat purred
and how the witch grinned,
As they sat on their broomstick
And flew through the wind.*

*But how the witch wailed
and how the cat spat,
When the wind blew so wildly
it blew off the hat.*

Loud and soft

The volume of a sound can have a profound effect. Loud sounds can at times excite, surprise, or scare us. We may hear softer sounds as soothing or spooky depending on the context in which they occur. Sometimes, it is the contrast—going from loud to soft and back again—that makes a piece of music particularly memorable.

neh-nah
neh-nah

brrmm
brrmm

woof
woof

la la la

tweet
tweet

1 Select a favorite poem. After reading it at your normal volume to your child, try it in a softer voice and then a louder one. Which does your child like best? Try the same activity with another poem to determine if different poems are better in different voices.

2 As you're playing at a park, stop for a minute's silence. Tell your child to listen carefully for any sounds that he can hear in that time. Make a list of the sounds and help your child to categorize them as either loud or soft. Repeat the exercise. This time, try to find more sounds for the softer side of the list—these are more difficult to hear.

3 Many cultures have imaginary characters that flit through scary stories—goblins, witches, and ghouls are just some of them. With your child, choose one of these characters and imagine the sounds that you think this imaginary creature would make. Are they soft sounds or loud sounds? If you change the sounds from soft to loud or loud to soft, does the effect change?

Another activity to try

Stand in your child's bedroom and look at the various items around the room. If you tapped different things together, would they be loud or soft? Ask your child to try tapping a pillow against the bed, a race car against the dresser, or a stuffed animal against the window. As long as nothing will break, anything is fair game!

Tip   Children love to yell. This natural inclination is not problematic in moderation, but if shouting starts to seem nonstop, encourage softer tones. Over a long period of time, excessive screeching can harm a child's voice.

Syllable sounds

Our language is made up of syllables using consonants (such as p, k, and t) and vowels (such as a, e, and o). By themselves, consonants can sound like percussion instruments—little bursts of sound that we can make—while vowels form the core of our speech. A child in early stages of language development benefits from explorations of speech and song, where the vowels are perfect for long and sustained phrases.

You will need

- Scarf
- Mirror

1 Stand in front of a mirror with your child. Choose a consonant, and watch the way the sound is made. How do the lips and the tongue move? When you make a "t" sound, for example, you can see your tongue touch the roof of your mouth to make the sound.

2 With your child, choose your favorite consonants and put them in an order: Chant them over and over again: "k-t-p / k-t-p / k-t-p." For an extra challenge, try to repeat each consonant in your pattern twice.

3 Take a deep breath and sing some vowels—for a long time—on any pitch. Put your hand lightly on your throat and feel the vibration. You can sing while your child feels the vibrations of your voice, or you can both sing and feel your own vibrations.

4 Singing long vowels and short vowels, wave the scarf through the air for the extent of the vowel sound. Raise the scarf up into the air at the start of your singing and bring it down when you stop. Practice this together.

5 Return to the mirror with your child. Notice how the mouth moves and takes on different shapes for the vowel sounds—the lips, jaw, tongue, and teeth.

Another activity to try

For children who are learning the letters of the alphabet, make connections to the visual representation of the letters.

The rhythms inside

Life's rhythms

Children are attracted to rhythms of all kinds—natural, mechanical, and within the music they hear and make. There is rhythm in the sounds we sing and play, and in the many objects that can be tapped, rattled, rung, patted, and plucked. This chapter is all about exploring rhythm through our voices, on musical instruments, and using familiar objects at home and outdoors. Your child will revel in inventing rhythms with the sounds that you find together.

In their earliest years, children show an engagement with rhythm in their speech and song, and through movement. They rhythmically sway, rock, and bounce at less than one year of age, and they babble in regular and irregular rhythmic patterns of phonemes and partial words before they can speak. By three to four years of age, children become increasingly conscious of the beat: It shows in their ways of walking and tapping on things, and in their love of rhymes that are rhythmic. By the age of five, a child may be internalizing the steady beat—even at various tempos. She can apply body percussion to the imitation of rhythms, and to the independent invention of rhythms on instruments.

This chapter considers the progression of a child from an awareness of fundamental speech rhythms to rhythms that are sounded in poetry, song, old-time clocks and watches; on recordings of music in a wide span of styles; and on kitchen items such as pots, pans, paper products, bowls, and buckets. You and your child can explore and enjoy rhythm inside and out, and the extent to which rhythm is alive in our daily doings will be brought home through the activities you share.

Tick-tock clock

Introduce your child to the steady tick-tock rhythm of a clock. Clocks regulate our days, providing the structure by which we know where we need to be, when we need to be. Time is also a core construct of music, where it is called tempo. Some songs have a fast tempo, others have a slow one, and still others switch in the middle. Sometimes, it is the varying of fast and slow that makes a particular piece of music memorable.

You will need

- Paper or index cards
- Crayons
- Friends or siblings

Tip It is not a problem if your child does not recognize numbers. Showing him the card while saying the number will help him learn them, even if it is unconscious.

Tick-tock clock *continued*

1 In a sing-song voice, make up a rhyme about the time: "Tick-tock, tick-tock, the time right now is 1 o'clock," while showing one finger. Repeat, but with 2 o'clock, moving all the way up to 10 o'clock.

2 Write the numbers 1 to 10 on different pieces of index card, and repeat the rhyme once more, this time showing the correct number on the card.

3 Using the same tick-tock poem, change the tempo. Try to say it very quickly, then try it slowly. Alternate between fast and slow. Draw an image of a clock on paper and invite your child to tap it as you recite the poem. With each tap, switch to a faster tempo or a slower one. Try switching roles with your child, so that each of you is able to be the "tempo conductor."

4 Play a singing game! Gather together a group of friends or siblings. One child acts as a wolf and stands alone, while the rest of the group stands roughly 15 feet (5 m) away. Together, the group choruses, "What time is it, Mr. Wolf?" and the wolf answers, "1 o'clock!" The group repeats the question, and the wolf replies, "2 o'clock!" Continue the pattern until 12 o'clock (or some other predetermined time), when the wolf yells, "12 o'clock! Supper time!" At this point, the wolf tries to tag as many children as he can for his evening meal.

Another activity to try

Find the different clocks and watches in your home, and put each one to your child's ear. Do they all tick? How are the ticks the same or different?

The beat goes on

An essential feature of most music, the beat is a regular and recurring rhythmic pulse. Whether strong or weak, the beat is characterized by its constant presence in the music. In a multisensory manner, the musical beat is heard as it is also felt. It regulates music, because it is the steady stress underlying a variety of other rhythms, melodies, and textures. Regardless of whatever else is apparent within music, the beat goes on and on.

You will need

- Spoons or chopsticks
- Plastic bowls

1 Sit face-to-face with your child and opposite one another so that, with arms outstretched, you hold hands. Begin to rock back and forth, and left and right. No music is necessary, as the beat is one that you and your child determine in the movement you make.

2 Rock to the beat while vocalizing. Try counting "one, two, three, four," or counting in another language "*uno, dos, tres, cuatro,*" or chanting the alphabet letters "*a-b-c-d.*" Play with the possibility of rhyming words on the beat, while you and your child alternate the words "cat-hat-mat-pat-chant-sat-mat-bat."

3 Settle the rocking down while starting to pat or tap heads and shoulders, tummies and toes. Do it while vocalizing words. You can be the patter-tapper, keeping the steady pulse with every touch.

4 Find something to pat and tap with, such as two spoons tapping together or chopsticks tapping plastic bowls. As you vocalize, play together by wrapping your child's hands with yours and feeling the motion of the hand make contact with the surface of the pot on the stronger and the weaker beats.

Other activities to try

Rock to the beat of a playlist of favorite musical selections. Compile the playlist in advance and include a variety of styles, each song about a half minute in length. They may be instrumental only or with a vocal part, children's or adult selections, from Beethoven to Beyoncé, and in faster or slower tempos.

Explore rhythm using Worksheet 3

Tip

For younger children, have the child sitting on your lap facing away from you, and start by cradling the child in your arms as you rock back and forth. You can turn your child to face you once you start vocalizing.

Rat-a-tat-tat

Drums come in all shapes and sizes and include those with skin stretched over a frame or shell and those whose drum heads are made of wood, as in plastic or rubber log drums. They can be played using hands or sticks. Occasionally, multiple sticks may be played by multiple players, as in the communal playing of a large bass drum by members of Plains Indian groups. The oldest known instrument in the world, as well as the most ubiquitous, the drum holds special appeal for children.

1 If using, turn plastic buckets upside down, so that the mouth is touching the floor and the base is facing upward.

2 While sitting on a chair in front of the drum, show your child how to try out the sound. Using two wooden dowels (or spoons), play hard, then soft, and short and then long. Play first at the sides of the drum, then find the "sweet sound" at the center.

3 Take turns playing the drum in a follow-the-leader manner, as first you and then your child take the lead in playing a phrase that the other imitates. To avoid the phrase becoming overly long—and potentially too challenging for your child to recall—play rhythms within an eight-beat count.

4 For the older child, while one player taps out a steady beat on the drum, the other player can improvise a pattern that also runs to eight beats.

Other activities to try

Choose recorded music to play to, minding the change of tempo and tuning to the rhythm patterns that are present.

- -

Try playing the drum with the hands rather than using wooden dowels or spoons.

Sounds to compare

Through playful experimentation, your child learns that sounds can be louder or softer, higher or lower, faster or slower. It is also well within her potential to listen carefully in order to be able to compare and match sounds. Still, this task is more complicated than it may seem and requires concentration to listen to one sound, hold that sound in the memory, and then match it to a second sound. This activity is hands-on and playful, yet it also stresses the need to listen up and logically think through a comparison of sounds.

You will need

- 12 identical plastic cups or yogurt pots
- Dried lentils, peas, and rice
- Masking or duct tape
- Glue

1 Make six identical shakers (see page 89–91), half-filling two with peas, two with rice, and two with lentils. Don't paint them, but leave them without distinguishing marks. Divide the pairs, so that you have three different shakers on either side of your child.

2 Facing your child, pick up any shaker from the left of your child, raise it to your ear, and shake to listen.

3 Now pick up a shaker from the right side of your child, raise it to the same ear, and shake to listen.

4 Return to the first shaker to check if it matches the sound. Keep trying the shakers on the right side until you find the matching sound. When you do, pair the shakers and put them in front of you. Continue until all the shakers are matched.

5 Invite your child to match and pair the sounds in the same way. Set out the shakers, so they are ready for your child to try the activity. Afterward, you might want to open the shakers to check that she was right.

Another activity to try

Increase the number of shakers until your child is matching up to six pairs of sounds. You could use sugar, coffee, and breakfast cereal in the shakers for new sounds.

Clink and clank

The sounds of familiar items include those that go "clink" and "clank." These are the sounds of ringing and jingling glass or ceramic (clink) or metal striking something solid (clank). Children are familiar with these sounds as aural components of their environment, as well as the objects that create them. It is well within their ability to imitate and invent rhythms with these tone colors in mind.

You will need

- Spoons (metal and wooden)
- Ceramic mugs or bowls
- Metal cups or pots
- Keys

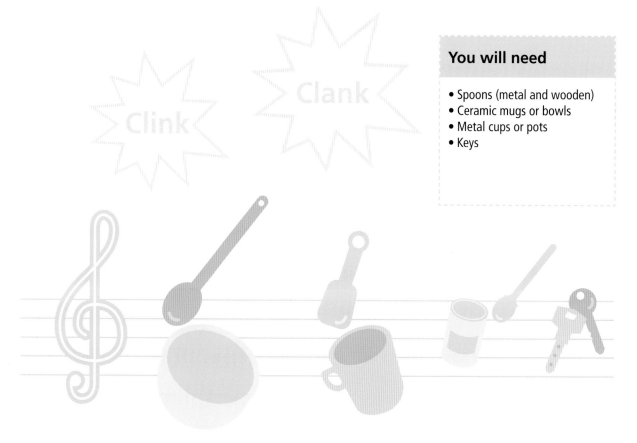

1 Explore the rhythmic sounds of wooden spoons against ceramic objects, and of metal spoons against metal objects. Encourage your child to clink wood on ceramic, and to clank metal on metal, freely.

2 Help your child to isolate the clink sounds, playing on these to make sounds that tingle, tinkle, and ring. Add a set of keys to the clink sound, jingling them.

3 Help your child to isolate the clank sounds, playing on these to make sounds that bong and clash.

4 See if the two of you can perform an eight-beat musical piece that features clinks and clanks and jangling keys. Try playing clinks on every beat, clanks on every other beat, and jingling keys on alternate beats as follows.

5 Repeat the eight-beat form to perfection. Then try playing loudly, then softly.

Tip

Note that the clinks and clanks are fairly close to one another, with clinks typically softer and higher and clanks noisier and a little lower.

Purr, ping, pop

Soft sounds are easily achieved using plastic objects or even wood on plastic. There may be a low "purring" vibration when scraping ridged plastic bottles, for example, or a short "pinging" or "popping" sound when tapping lids, cups, or plates of plastic.

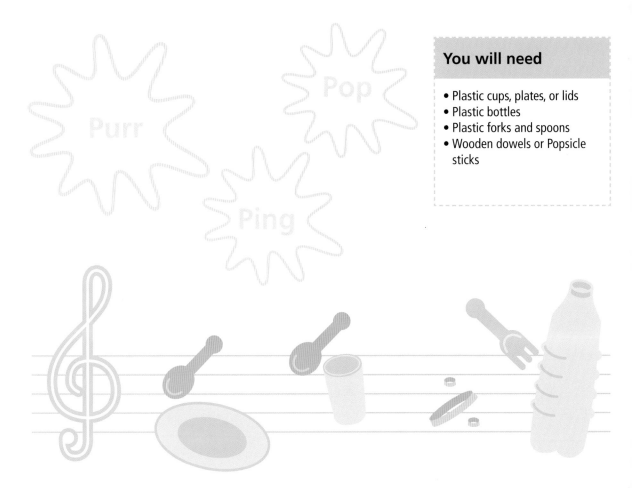

You will need

- Plastic cups, plates, or lids
- Plastic bottles
- Plastic forks and spoons
- Wooden dowels or Popsicle sticks

1 Encourage your child to experiment with the rhythmic ways in which various plastic objects can be tapped, knocked, or scraped. Tell her to listen for sounds that "purr" (especially if a ridged surface is scraped), or that "ping" or "pop" as a result of a sharp and short tap to an upside-down plastic cup, plate, or lid.

Other activities to try

Select recorded music of various styles, and tap your plastic objects to the rhythm of the beat.

- -

See if your child can add an ostinato rhythm to a piece of recorded music—that is, playing on every other beat, or playing two taps for every beat.

2 Show your child how to play eight steady beats on a ridged plastic bottle using a plastic fork or spoon, a wooden dowel, or a Popsicle stick.

3 With the mouth of a plastic cup facing down, show your child how to strike the surface of a table or the floor eight times (for eight beats).

4 Tap a plastic plate or lid with a plastic fork, a wooden dowel, or a Popsicle stick, sounding out eight beats. Invite your child to copy you.

5 Together, see if you can play a plastic piece with all of its purrs, pings, and pops, based on an eight-beat phrase that is repeated four times, as follows.

Bottle:	◆	—	◆	◆	◆	—	◆	—
Cup:	/	/	/	/	/	/	/	/
Plate / lid:	—	●	●	●	—	●	●	●

Say-and-play word chants

Speech rhythms are fundamental to music making. In many places in the world, syllables are associated with rhythms and are spoken in learning rhythms that may later be applied to instruments. Children enjoy vocalizing rhythms with words or syllables that may be semantically meaningless (such as "fa-la-la"). They speak and then play rhythmically with word chants (and syllable chants).

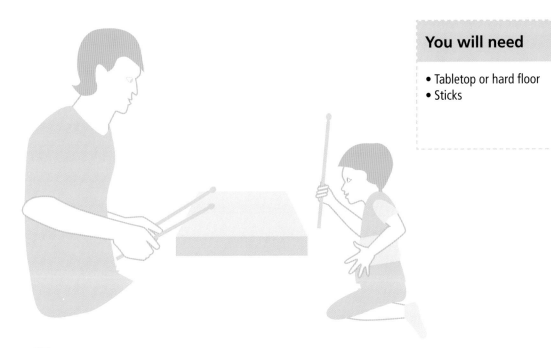

You will need

- Tabletop or hard floor
- Sticks

1 Choose a word with one syllable, such as *door* or *ball*. Say it in a steady rhythm, one word per beat: "Door – Door – Door – Door" or "Ball – Ball – Ball – Ball." Ask your child to join in.

2 Repeat the one-syllable words while tapping a tabletop or surface of a hard floor. Pick up two sticks—wooden or metal spoons, pencils, or pens are all good—to strike together while saying the word. Invite your child to tap the beat on the tabletop.

3 Now choose a word with two syllables, such as *apple* or *window*. Say it in a steady rhythm that is twice as fast as *door* or *ball*. In other words, the two-syllable words can be spoken in one beat, the same amount of time as the one-syllable words: "Ap-ple – Ap-ple – Win-dow – Win-dow." Ask your child to join in.

4 As in Step 2, say the two-syllable words while your child taps a tabletop or surface of a hard floor, and you play each syllable on sticks or other objects.

5 Mix and match the words to say and play: "Door – Door – Ap-ple – Door" or "Ball – Win-dow – Win-dow – Ball." With you holding two sticks and your child with just one, see if you can tap the beat on the tabletop—you playing the two-syllable words and your child tapping the one-syllable words.

6 Once your child has mastered the rhythm, encourage him to say the words silently as you repeat the rhythms together one more time.

Other activities to try

Build rhythms using people's names, such as Sean, Anne, Max, Jack and Em-ma, Ry-an, Lu-cas, Li-ly.

- -

Use one-syllable and two-syllable words in another language—for example, French **pain** (bread), **lait** (milk), **banane** (banana), and **citron** (lemon).

- -

Replace the sticks with objects made from different materials for a range of tone colors. Include objects of wood, metal, rubber, and plastic.

Rhyming in rhythm

Children delight in rhymes—those phrases that end with similar sounds. Short phrases, such as, "We ride our balloon all the way to the moon," are rhymed in ways that feel rhythmic. Poetry is filled with such rhymes that are rhythmically spoken. Alongside the fun of rhyming couplets and short poems, there is a strong link between rhythmically performed rhymes and memory. Rhythmic rhymes are often used as memory aids for ideas.

You will need

- Large sheet of thick paper
- Crayons
- Poetry (books, collections)

1 Choose a word and rhyme it, going through the alphabet to find first letters that make sense (or no sense at all). Say the words aloud to your child, keeping to a steady beat. For example: Words that rhyme with *blue*: Boo!, coo, clue, crew, do, dew, goo, glue, who, loo, moo!, new, ooh!, rue, sue, too, true, you, whoo!, zoo. Words that rhyme with *top*: Bop!, cop, drop, hop, mop, pop, stop.

2 Design an alphabet chart with crayons on paper to help your child find consonants of the alphabet for discovering rhymes, or make and decorate a card for each letter.

3 Make up some short rhyming couplets for your child to repeat after you. As each of you speaks, pat the beat on your lap or other surface.

4 Find books by Dr. Seuss (*The Cat in the Hat*, *Green Eggs and Ham*, *How the Grinch Stole Christmas*) and by Shel Silverstein (*Where the Sidewalk Ends*, *A Light in the Attic*, *The Giving Tree*). Read them aloud to your child, and in rhythm, to give a full aural sense of the rhyming words. Pat the beat to the rhythm.

5 Referring to the alphabet chart or cards that you made in Step 2, choose some rhyming word pairs and say them in rhythm. Then, use them to make two short sentences to create rhyming couplets. For example, for "mine" and "sign": *Please be mine. Give me a sign.* Repeat these newly invented rhymes in rhythm, with your child, and with both of you patting the beat to the poetic rhythm.

Other activities to try

Find other ways of showing your child the rhythm of the rhymes in the body. Beyond patting the beat, try walking the rhythmic rhymes or swaying to them.

Explore rhyme further using Worksheet 4.

Shake it up

Groove is something that children naturally understand. They may not be able to explain it, but when a pulsive rhythm track comes on—especially on drums and electric bass—a child manifests an innate desire to move to the beat. Rhythmic grooves are short rhythm patterns, and they are heard in music from jazz to reggae, and from rhythm and blues (R&B) to hip-hop.

You will need

- Music recordings of high-driving rhythms

1 Assemble a set of recordings of high-driving rhythms featuring a range of artists and musical styles. Choose them by listening to each with your child and asking the question, "Does it make us want to move and groove?" When the answer is yes, place the track in a queue of recordings.

2 Sitting down, pat the beat or the short repeated rhythm on your lap while listening to a tune.

3 Clear a space for dancing. Try out some moves with your child, beginning with the feet planted solidly on the floor and nodding your heads back and forth.

4 Try some groove moves, as follows, demonstrating each to your child before inviting her to join you:
• Up in the air: Pull your body up straight and tall while nodding and popping the head.
• Moving down: Bending and unbending the knees, changing from full to three-quarter height.
• Bounce: Jumping in place or in a small leap.
• Drop: Dropping down in a slight jump from full height to about half height.

5 Combine these moves to the groove music. Invent new moves, too, and notice how the repeated groove rhythm seems to suggest patterns of movement.

Tip
■ Be sure that toys and various other objects are off the floor and out of the way.
■ Small carpets may slide, so remove them to prevent slippage.

Our daily melodies

Tuneful times

Melody involves the rise and fall of pitch or tone, from high to higher, from low to lower. It is often repeated or gently undulating. Children are wrapped in the melodies of lullabies, and in the music of spoken and sung inflections that surround them on a daily basis. Instruments sound high and low—as do voices—and their melodies may run fast or slow, loud or soft. The following activities provide occasions for you and your child to play with the idea of "taking pitch for a walk"—up, down, and all around—and offer creative ways in which to celebrate the melodies that make our hearts sing.

Pitch is a reality in our everyday world. You can hear it in the inflections of speech—people use higher pitches in the energy of exciting topics and lower pitches in low-energy, everyday speech. When it comes to singing, playing, and listening, children in the three-to-five age range grow in their ability to recognize familiar phrases and songs based on the contour of successive pitches in a melody. As they make their way from four to five years of age, they can discriminate high and low pitches and the upward and downward movement of a melody.

The discovery of melody comes through vocal play, by singing nursery songs and games, by listening to recorded music, and through the music we make up. Melodies rise up from the experiences we have had, and children often compose songs that sound similar to the melody of a familiar lullaby or recording. Some of the most tuneful melodies are made by children engaged in water play and who sing on rainy days or days full of sunshine. Melody and pitch possibilities are also apparent in activities that feature combs, bowls, and bottles, and—not surprisingly—in explorations of the piano or keyboard.

Rainy-day play

Rain is essential to the ongoing growth of our planet. Watching rain stream down a windowpane can be a mesmerizing experience for a youngster, and children can be found blowing warm breath onto a window in order to draw in the condensation that follows. Once outside, children love nothing more than splashing around in puddles. Various sounds are associated with rainstorms as well, from the quietness of a drizzle to the howling of the wind to the booming of thunder.

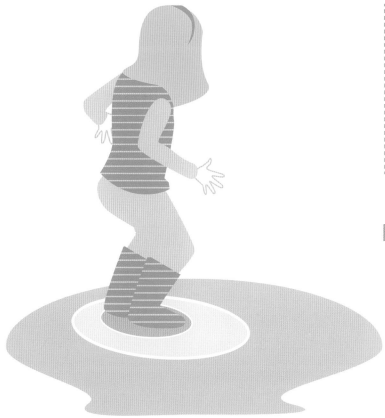

You will need

- Drum
- Lids of pots or pans
- Raincoats
- Waterproof shoes

1 If your child feels trapped indoors by the rain, turn the experience into a positive one. Make a dramatic rainstorm for her using only your hands.

Rainy-day play *continued*

2 Try the following sequence: Rub your hands together; tap your fingers on your lap; pat your hands softly on your lap; pat your hands loudly on your lap; if standing, stamp on the floor.

3 Once your rainstorm has reach full blast, reverse the order of movements, ending with your hands rubbing together. Encourage your child to join in with you.

4 Add thunder to your rainstorm. Consider a variety of ways to make a thunder-like sound: playing a drum, crashing the lids of two pots or pans together, or yelling "crash!" will all work. As you create the rainstorm with your hands, encourage your child to make the thunder roar. Use the terms *loud* and *soft* to discuss the different sounds you're making.

Tip   For adults, becoming wet is a hassle, but for many children, playing in the rain is the height of excited fun. Plan ahead with dry clothes, so that as soon as you finish, you can warm up. A warm cup of tea or hot chocolate isn't a bad idea, either!

5 Play with puddles! Put on a raincoat and galoshes and head outside, looking for the biggest puddles around. Use your feet to tap the edge of a puddle; do it softly at first, then add more force. After noting that the splash certainly gets larger, ask your child to identify how the sound changes.

6 If you can find a deep enough puddle, swipe a branch through the water, sending up a wave. What does it sound like? Consider replacing the stick with your hand, making a bigger wave. Then go home to change out of your wet clothes.

Other activities to try

Seek out Beethoven's "Pastoral Symphony" and listen for the different sounds that make up the storm movement.

Make up a short song about rain, using your child's name: "Rain, rain, go away, come again another day. Little Mary wants to play. Rain, rain, go away!" Ask your child to describe an outdoor activity she would like to do if it were not raining, and repeat the song. Repeat until you run out of ideas.

Singing our rhymes

Rhymes can be spoken or sung. They simply involve the repetition of sound in two or more words, as in *sing* and *ring* and *cat* and *sat*. Rhyming words often feature as the final syllables in two sentences or phrases. Familiar to young children are nursery rhymes that tend to be transmitted orally over the generations in one complete package of poetic verse, rhythm, and melody.

You will need

• Nursery rhymes

Nursery rhymes

These melodies have been selected from the collection known as *Mother Goose Rhymes*.

Twinkle, Twinkle, Little Star
Twinkle, twinkle, little star.
How I wonder what you are!
Up above the world so high,
Like a diamond in the sky.
Twinkle, twinkle, little star,
How I wonder what you are!

Baa Baa Black Sheep
Baa baa black sheep, Have you any wool?
Yes sir, yes sir, Three bags full.
One for the Master, One for the Dame,
One for the little boy who lives down the lane.

Rain, Rain, Go Away
Rain, rain, go away,
Come again another day.
Little Suzy wants to play.
Rain, rain, go away.

Itsy Bitsy Spider
The itsy bitsy spider went up the water spout.
Down came the rain and washed the spider out.
Out came the sun and dried up all the rain,
And the itsy bitsy spider went up the spout again.

1. Sit with your child on your lap, facing toward you. Sing a favorite nursery rhyme to him. A number of popular nursery rhymes are offered here (see opposite page). Perhaps they will trigger your memory or offer new rhyme potentials.

Another activity to try

Use Worksheet 5 for your child to list his favorite songs.

2. As you sing the songs, increase the volume of the rhyming words at the end of each phrase.

3. Sing the songs again (and again), and play with possible gestures to represent the words. Some standard gestures include raising the hands above the head, fingers spread (for *Twinkle, Twinkle, Little Star*) and taking thumb to index finger and connecting the two hands in the shape of a spider (*Itsy Bitsy Spider*).

4. Encourage your child to hand-clap the beat, and try alternating between clapping your own hands and clapping those of your child.

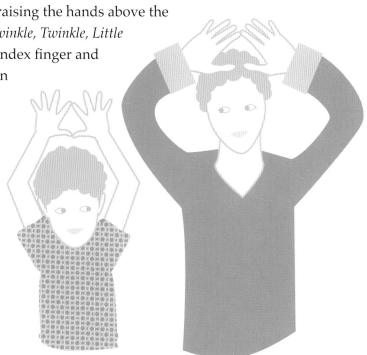

Song of the vegetables

With an understanding that a carrot is healthier than potato chips, and that celery beats sweets for nutrition, a song can be a powerful carrier of a message that encourages children to follow a balanced diet. Why simply say, "Eat your veggies!" when you can sing about it together? By putting a rhythm and a melody to words of encouragement, children may fast develop an interest in the food that is good for them.

You will need

- Several cleaned vegetables (carrot, cucumber, lettuce, green beans, green pepper)
- Wooden spoons
- Cutting board
- Knife
- Small bowls

Nursery rhymes

Create short verses with a rhythmic swing. Here are two verses that might appeal to your child, or you can have fun making up your own:

*Veggies are wonderfully good
  for me.
They give me lots of my energy!
They have Vitamin B and
  Vitamin C,
And some of them give me my
  Vitamin D.*

*Give me a carrot, a pepper
  that's green,
And a skinny and stringy and
  very long bean.
Cucumber slices like saucers
  in air,
Broccoli bushes and lettuce
  so fair.*

1 Start by making up a song with your child. Choose as your focus veggies that your child particularly likes. If he prefers fruits to veggies, use those instead. Select words that focus on taste, color, crunching sounds, juice—whatever appeals to him. We have suggested a song you might want to use (see right).

2 Once you have made up the song, repeat it, asking your child to pick up, or point to, the vegetables as you describe them. You can place the veggies in a row or jumble them up for a more challenging activity.

3 Keeping the verse rhythmic, invite your child to join you in chanting the verses over and again.

4 Tap the tabletop while chanting the verses together, giving emphasis to the rhymed syllables. Use either your fingertips or wooden spoons rhythmically. Encourage your child to follow suit.

Tip
- Young children should not be entrusted with a real knife; make sure they understand why.
- Be sure that your child fully chews each vegetable chunk before beginning again.

5 Insert this phrase at the beginning of the song, between the verses, and at the close: "No. More. Junk. Food." Note how the punctuation encourages you to speak the phrase more slowly, in comparison to the more rhythmic flow of the sung verses.

6 Using a safe chopping knife, begin to chop the vegetables one by one into bite-size chunks. You should do the chopping, using an action that is regular and steady. Invite your child to keep tapping the tabletop in order to help you keep to the beat.

7 As you chop, place the chunks from each vegetable into a separate small bowl. This time, as you chant the verses once more, pause at every vegetable to allow your child to have a taste.

8 Be sure to allow time for your child to chew each vegetable fully and swallow before moving on. In order for this to happen, you might improvise on the phrase, "No. More. Junk. Food," or any other phrase, such as, "Veggies are wonderfully good for me."

9 Continue tapping the beat throughout the whole activity.

Other activities to try

Try giving your vegetables stimulating nicknames like X-ray Vision Carrot, Flying Saucer Cucumber, and Enchanted Forest Broccoli Bush.

Eat your vegetables along with your child to model healthy eating habits.

Water music

Children enjoy water play, and water offers a unique pathway for musical exploration. With hands or whole selves in the water, children will splish, splash, and play in a tub. Water also has a way of loosening children up to sing, and water is a frequent topic of folk and popular songs through the ages.

You will need

- Large sink; pot or pan; bathtub; small pool; or safe water zone in river, lake, or sea.
- Rubber duck, small boat, or other rubber water toys

1 As your child enters the water—hands alone or whole self—allow some time for free play of the hands and arms (and feet, legs, and torso). Notice the rhythm of the movement, and listen for any vocal expression— expect squeals of delight, giggles, or even full-out laughter. There may even be some singing to join in on.

Tip
- Never leave the area of water play unsupervised, even if it is a bathtub or pool.
- Be ready with a dry towel if your child gets water in his eyes or feels cold. Have dry clothes ready, too.
- If the water play venue is outside, have sunscreen available.

Water music *continued*

2 With your arms in the water, invite your child to choose a water toy, and select one for yourself. Play together, moving the toys back and forth—in lines, zigzags, circles, and figure eights. Play follow-the-leader, taking turns in moving the toys following a particular pattern.

3 Sing freely, or vocalize in some way (chant, hum) parts of familiar melodies. Make up tunes to words as they come naturally. Notice how the music you make will match the movement of your hands.

4 Tell your child a story that features the bath toys as they interact. For example, develop dramatic or sung dialogue of a rubber duck who has an injury and needs a boat ride to the other side of the lake, or of two rubber ducks who were first afraid of each other but develop a strong friendship together (see box at right for more ideas).

5 End the water play with another period of free time. Play the orchestral suite of short entertainment pieces called "Water Music" by G. F. Handel. Watch the way in which your child responds to the rhythm, flow, and spirit of the strings, horns, trumpets, flutes, recorders, oboes, bassoons, and basses.

Story ideas

Depending on the bath toys you have, your stories might involve:

A deep-sea diver who discovers a shipwreck with buried treasure

A mother duck who plays hide-and-seek with her ducklings

Fishermen whose boat survives stormy weather and wash up on an unknown island

Other activities to try

Design a playlist of songs in which water is the principal topic. Include such favorites as "The Water Is Wide," "Old Man River," "The Rio Grande," "Shenandoah," "Blow the Man Down," "Botany Bay," "Big Boat up the River," "The Erie Canal," and "Roll On Columbia." Popular music has its share, too, such as Otis Redding's image-laden "Sittin' on the Dock of the Bay."

Play the songs often, and watch how you and your child learn them by heart and even dance to them.

Rock-a-bye lullabies

Lullabies are meaningful to children and adults alike. Their soft, undulating melodies are just right for smoothing the active mind at the close of a busy day, or for a short midday nap. Soothing melodies, gentle rhythms, and the sound of a familiar voice make for memorable times that communicate safety, security, and tender loving care.

You will need

- Soft stuffed animal or doll
- Rocking chair (optional)

1 Choose a lullaby, either one featured on these pages or another family favorite.

2 If there is a rocking chair available, sit in it with your child. Begin singing the lullaby while rocking the chair back and forth to a gentle and regular beat.

3 Invite your child to cradle a favorite soft stuffed toy in her arms—a teddy bear, toy dog, cat, or doll—just as you would have cradled her as a baby.

4 Show her how to move her arms gently from side to side in a rocking manner as you sing the lullaby together.

Favorite lullabies

Rock-a-Bye Baby
Rock-a-bye baby, on the treetop,
When the wind blows, the cradle will rock.
When the bough breaks, the cradle will fall,
And down will come baby, cradle and all.

You Are My Sunshine
You are my sunshine, my only sunshine.
You make me happy when skies are gray.
You'll never know, dear, how much I love you.
Please don't take my sunshine away.

Hush, Little Baby
Hush, little baby, don't say a word, Papa's gonna buy you a
*   mockingbird.*
And if that mockingbird don't sing, Papa's gonna buy you a
*   diamond ring.*
And if that diamond ring turns brass, Papa's gonna buy you a
*   looking glass.*
And if that looking glass gets broke, Papa's gonna buy you a
*   billy goat.*
And if that billy goat don't pull, Papa's gonna buy you a cart
*   and bull.*
And if that cart and bull turn over, Papa's gonna buy you a
*   dog named Rover.*
And if that dog named Rover won't bark, Papa's gonna buy
*   you a horse and cart.*
And if that horse and cart fall down, You'll still be the
*   sweetest little baby in town.*

Comb music

It is remarkable just how many items in the home can make music. A simple comb used to untangle or style hair is a great item from which to make an instrument. Made of plastic, sometimes metal, its row of narrow teeth can feel good to flick forward with the thumb, thus making a subtle sound of rising or falling pitches. Better yet, use a sheet of wax paper or tissue to convert your comb into a homemade buzzy kazoo.

You will need

- Combs
- Wax paper or tissue

Tip Although the comb teeth are covered with paper, it is wise to clean or sterilize them before taking them to the mouth.

1 Take a comb into your hand and invite your child to do the same. With your child watching, push your thumb across the tiny teeth, all in one direction. Listen to the pitches together and decide if they are rising up or falling down. Play a few rhythm patterns for your child by flicking the teeth of the comb, and encourage him to do the same.

2 Place a piece of tissue or wax paper over the tooth edge of your comb. Hum a familiar tune through the tissue or wax paper, and listen to the sound.

3 Make a second comb instrument in the same way for your child. Invite him to hum the same tune. Compare the sounds of the two combs.

4 Play imitatively, with one person leading and the other repeating. Try also a call-and-response form, in which one person creates a melodic pattern and another person answers with a different pattern.

Another activity to try

For an older child, decide that one comb will play rhythm and another will play melody. Create a little comb music together.

Bottles and bowls

Children are intrigued with the way that the amount of water in a vessel affects the sound waves, or pitch, when that vessel is tapped. A group of eight (or even just five) bottles or bowls function a little like a xylophone, in that one pitch is higher than the one before it, in a full lineup. All sorts of songs—from "Lightly Row" and "Jingle Bells" to Beethoven's "Ode to Joy"—can be played using such a lineup. In interesting ways, this project combines mathematical measurements, music, and the physics of sound.

Tip   The sound of a metal spoon to glass is very attractive but should be approached with caution for fear of breakage by an energetic young child.

1 Line up the eight bottles, beakers, or bowls.

2 Fill the first vessel about one-eighth full of water for the highest note. Fill the second glass about one-quarter (two-eighths) full, the third glass about three-eighths full, and so on.

3 Each vessel should sound like a note on the scale, from the fullest—the low Do—through Re, Mi, Fa, So, La, Ti, and the high Do (the least full of all vessels). Adjust the water level to tune the scale pitches more accurately.

4 Play the scale with a wooden spoon or dowel. Demonstrate the scale first for your child, and then let her play it herself. Allow her to practice a number of times.

5 Sing along while figuring out the melodies for some of the songs your child likes—for example, "Row, Row, Row Your Boat," "Mary Had a Little Lamb," and "Twinkle, Twinkle, Little Star."

Other activities to try

Add food coloring to the water in the vessels to help identify the pitches of the scale.

Play a pentatonic scale by removing the fourth and seventh vessel, leaving the pitches low Do, Re, Mi, So, La, and high Do. This pitch set works well for many melodies from China, Japan, and Korea, as well as for many Anglo-American tunes.

For an older child, jumble the order of the vessels and ask her to reorder them correctly based only on the pitch she hears as you strike each of them.

Piano music

The piano stands as one of the world's most easily recognized instruments, with its large body and distinctive black and white keys. After many hours and years of practice, professional pianists can coax remarkable sounds from this instrument. With supervision, young children can also make a variety of sounds that can entice and inspire their creativity.

You will need

- A piano, keyboard, or piano computer app

1 Using just one finger at a time, take "baby steps" to climb the piano keys, moving note by note from the bottom to the top, and then back down again. Then, try "giant leaps," where your fingers make larger jumps up and down the piano keys. Do this several times with your child watching, then suggest that he turns around so that the piano is no longer in view. Repeat the exercise, asking your child to identify whether you are making baby steps or giant leaps.

2 Children love making up songs, particularly on an instrument like a piano. Set your child free, with one important guideline—never to bang on a piano. Settle him on a chair and let him freely explore the keys. His "song" likely won't have much interest to you, but his free-form plunkings can be evocative for him.

3 Choose a favorite picture book that has two or three characters recurring throughout the story. For each character, make up a short musical pattern (just two or three seconds) using only the black keys. Read the book, and every time each character is mentioned, play his or her "theme."

Other activities to try

Sing one of your favorite children's songs, and try to sound it out for your child on the piano. You can try to figure out the correct notes, and your child can be the judge, telling you if you are correct in your performance.

Use Worksheet 7 to encourage your child to make drawings of his favorite instruments.

Music at home

Found sounds and musical instruments

There are many sources for making music with children in the home. Sometimes the music arises spontaneously from a child—at a spur-of-a-joyful moment in the kitchen, the bedroom, or the bathroom, for example. We also find ourselves intentionally making time for gathering potential sound sources for playful music-making experiences or calling on treasured music played at special occasions. This chapter provides activities to help you make music with your child at home, using accessible sound sources, for both everyday and special occasions.

Open the kitchen cabinets, and what do you have? Plentiful sound sources—found sounds that can be drawn from the likes of wooden and metal spoons on pots, pans, kettles, and woks. There are plastic eggs, cups, yogurt containers, and soda cans waiting to be filled with rice and macaroni as musical shakers. You can fit paper plates with jingle bells to make homemade tambourines or use an empty box as the base of a rubber-band guitar.

In other places and times of home and family life, there are wonderful opportunities to surround your child with music: as he awakes, when he naps, while he is sleeping. There is holiday music to listen to, or to sing, play, and dance to. With siblings or friends, your child can experience the joy of making something beautiful—a song by a makeshift "choir" or instrumental sounds on an ensemble of real and homemade instruments. Perhaps he'll rise to the chance of putting on a show that dramatizes a story and becomes more magical with the addition of familiar and newly made music.

Kitchen music

The kitchen is often the heart of the family home, the hub of activity for children and adults alike. It is the location of a full supply of food, and of the pots and pans in which the food is prepared. Whether you have a heavy-duty cast-iron skillet or a light-as-aluminum boiling pot, cookware can be appealing to a young child. With little effort, he can bang, crash, ding, ring, tinkle, and zing—especially with the help of a wooden spoon.

You will need

- Pots
- Pans
- Tea kettles
- Woks
- Wooden or metal spoons

Kitchen music *continued*

1 Gather together a selection of kitchen pans and pots, and include a tea kettle and wok, too, if you have them on hand.

2 Using a wooden spoon, tap on the side, the rim, and the top (if there is a metal lid) of each piece of cookware. Turn the cookware upside down and tap on it. Invite your child to do the same. Ask him to experiment by tapping with a metal spoon, too.

3 Work with your child to find, in all of the cookware assembled, the highest pitch and the lowest pitch, the brightest tone and the darkest tone.

4 Tap a steady beat on just one pot or pan, and invite your child to join you. Switch parts, so that your child may initiate a steady beat—at any speed—on which you can join in playing. You may wish to sing a familiar song as you tap the beat.

5 In follow-the-leader fashion, play short four-beat patterns that your child can easily imitate. After four or five short patterns, switch roles so your child becomes the leader.

Tip   The sound of metal on metal—especially with very large pots and pans—can sometimes hurt the ears. Use metal utensils sparingly, and opt more often for wooden spoons.

6 Now add more pots and pans in various shapes and sizes that will produce a wide span of metallic sounds. Repeat Steps 4 and 5 to practice—first a steady beat, then imitation of short phrases. This time, notice the diversity of pitches and tone colors you can create for a more interesting sound palette.

7 Invent a duet of kitchen sounds, with the goal of playing and listening to what can be created together. Clarify that each player can play on the beat, or with short repeated patterns, and that it is also fine to rest and listen while the other plays.

Other activities to try

Challenge your child to listen longer by extending the length of the patterns for imitation in Step 5 from four beats to eight beats.

In creating music together, talk about possibilities for variation by choosing to play loud or soft, or fast or slow, or with bright or darker tones.

Ocean drums

For centuries, people have enjoyed the sounds of rain sticks and ocean drums. Such instruments are found in the Pacific Islands (Hawaii, Samoa, and Fiji, for example); among indigenous Australians; and in Peruvian, Chilean, Mexican, and ancient Aztec cultures. They are gently shaken, or given a little more energy in the shake, to create the sound of falling rain or ocean waves lapping the shore. For people in some cultures, the sound is welcomed as a method that sustains fish in the water, animals, and crops. To others, it provides a relaxing or meditative quality.

You will need

- Small box
- Utility knife
- Acetate sheet
- Scissors
- Masking or duct tape
- Small pasta shapes or dried beans
- Paints and colorful construction paper

1 Gather the materials together. Consider making two instruments—one for you and one for your child.

2 To make each ocean drum, use a utility knife to cut a window in the top of the box, so that your child will be able to see the pasta or beans moving inside the instrument as it is tipped. The window can be small or large.

3 Use scissors to cut a piece of acetate, ensuring that it is 2 in (5 cm) larger than the cutout window on the top of the box.

4 Place the cut plastic over the cutout window of the box, and secure it using masking or duct tape.

5 Fill the box with 20 to 30 pieces of small pasta or dried beans.

6 Seal the drum tightly with masking or duct tape.

7 Invite your child to help you decorate the box with paints. Tape colorful construction paper over any words on the packaging.

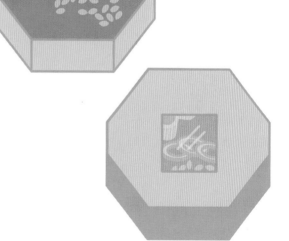

Tip Cutting the box with a utility knife is most certainly an adult endeavor. Keep all knives and scissors (except small, child-safe scissors) out of reach of little ones.

Ocean drums *continued*

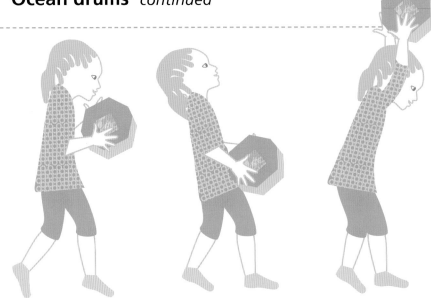

8 Encourage your child to play the drum. Show her how to tilt it one way and then the other, and tell her to listen to the rolling sound of the contents.

9 As your child becomes familiar with the instrument, show her how the sounds become slower and faster depending on the degree of the tilt.

10 Experiment with different types of sound—those that are rhythmically free and reflective and those that are regular in keeping a musical pulse.

Other activities to try

Try playing the drum with music, especially music from the Pacific Islands such as Hawaii, Samoa, and Fiji.

If you have made two boxes, establish a follow-the-leader game, in which you join in with the music first and your child copies your rhythm.

Rattle and roll

From their earliest days of having rattles in the crib, children enjoy the sound of a shaker. They go by various names, including the Latin American maracas that are present in music in Brazil, Cuba, Mexico, Puerto Rico, Venezuela, and elsewhere across the Caribbean and in Central and South America. Maracas are hollow balls made from dried gourd shells filled with dried beans, and your child will love making versions of his own shakers to rattle and roll.

You will need

- Plastic containers (two yogurt containers or two cups)
- Rice, macaroni, dried beans, or peas
- Masking or duct tape
- Glue
- Paint (acrylic) or colorful fabric strips

1 Gather the materials together and choose two identical containers to form the base of your instrument.

2 Fill each container about one-quarter full with rice, macaroni, dried beans, or peas. Invite your child to help you do this.

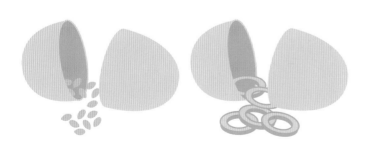

3 Close up the containers. You may find that some containers can simply be taped shut, while others need to be glued first and then taped together.

4 Either way, wrap more masking or duct tape around where the containers join together for added support.

5 Allow your child to personalize his shakers, painting them in bright colors or gluing colorful fabric strips over the surfaces.

6 Make as many shakers as you have materials for, and allow them to dry fully before using.

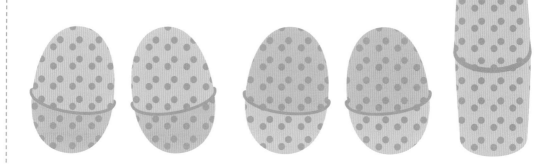

7 When it comes to making music, show your child how to play the shakers. Take one in each hand and demonstrate by flicking your wrists in a quick downward motion.

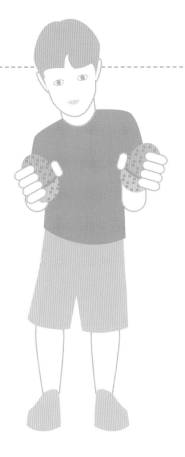

Other activities to try

While making the instruments, listen to Latin American music (including recordings by Machito, Benny Moré, Buena Vista Social Club, and Glen Velez) that features maracas. This music will surely motivate your young instrument maker to complete the project.

For the older child, use a blindfold to see if he can distinguish the sounds made by the different materials in the shakers—rice, macaroni, dried beans, or peas.

8 Once your child has practiced shaking the instruments for himself, encourage him to alternate hands, shaking one and then the other. Tell him to shake slowly at first and then to pick up the speed.

9 Take a pair of shakers yourself and experiment with your child, playing different rhythms. Start with even, single beats and gradually work up to two shakes within a single beat.

10 Shake the shakers to a variety of musical recordings.

Tooting our horns

Horns are alive and well in many places in the world. While the beautifully coiled brass instrument known as the French horn sounds in symphonies and chamber music groups, there are also animal horns that are still used in various societies to sound out signals and melodies. Your child can express herself both artistically and musically in the process of making and then performing on her very own horns of household materials.

You will need

- Tubes from paper towel or toilet paper rolls
- Wax paper
- Rubber band
- Pen
- Paints

1 From the collected materials, take a tube and a piece of wax paper about twice the size of the tube opening. Use the paper to cover just one end of the tube, securing it with a rubber band.

2 Punch small holes in the wax paper using the tip of a pen. This is something you could ask your child to do.

3 Invite your child to decorate the horn's tube with brightly colored designs. Make a number of tubes in this way—at least one for each of you.

4 Show your child how to play the horn by vocalizing into it. Say "toot" repeatedly, in any rhythms that come to mind. Encourage your child to copy you.

5 Try a call-and-response form of music making, with one horn sounding an opening call and the other horn responding (not necessarily in imitation but in a personally inventive manner).

6 Show your child how singing through the horn makes it function like a megaphone.

Other activities to try

For inspiration, listen to French horn recordings such as Tchaikovsky's "5th Symphony" (horn solo) and Richard Strauss's "Concerto No. 1" for French horn.

Listen also to animal horn sounds from cows, longhorn sheep, deer, antelope, gazelle, elk, and kudu.

Use Worksheet 8 to explore a range of instrumental music.

Rubber-band guitar

The guitar is one of the most popular musical instruments in the world. A member of the lute family of instruments, the guitar consists of a body, an extended neck, and a number of strings. Children enjoy the lively sound of music that features guitars, be it blues, bluegrass, country, flamenco, mariachi, reggae, and many more forms of popular music.

You will need

- Cardboard box (for shoes or tissues)
- Utility knife
- 6 long, thick rubber bands
- 2–3 in (5–7.5 cm) stick or ruler
- Craft glue
- Masking or duct tape
- Paints

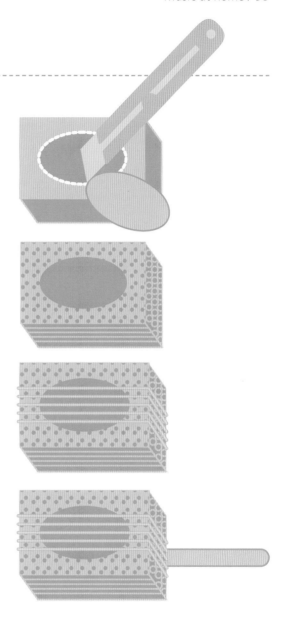

1. Take a cardboard box and—if it does not have one already—cut a hole in the center using a utility knife. In the case of a shoe box, remove the lid to do this. For a tissue box, remove the plastic around the hole.

2. Invite your child to paint the box in bright colors or with designs that may include dots, spots, stripes, and stars.

3. Stretch the rubber bands over the hole from one end of the box to the other. Space them evenly so they do not touch one another.

4. Use glue to paste a long, flat stick (or ruler) to the back of the box to serve as the neck of the instrument. Reinforce the bond with masking or duct tape.

Rubber-band guitar *continued*

5 Show your child how to strum and pluck the rubber bands to produce sound. You can adjust the tuning by pulling the rubber bands tighter or looser and securing them in place with tape.

6 Encourage your child to strum in a rhythmic way to a steady beat with a downstroke:

or to create a simple rhythm that combines downstrokes with upstrokes:

7 Help your child to devise a pattern to pluck using the index finger: It may involve all six rubber bands or perhaps fewer, selected bands. Tell him to pluck using a regular steady-beat rhythm.

Other activities to try

Motivate your child in his making of a rubber-band guitar by playing music of great guitarists like B. B. King, Carlos Santana, Django Reinhardt, Jimi Hendrix, Paco de Lucía, Robert Johnson, and Andrés Segovia.

- - - - - - - - - - - - - - - - -

Invite an older child to play along in strums and plucks with recordings of these guitarists, catching their rhythms (if not their chords and melodies).

Shake that tambourine

Tambourines are famous for the joyful expressions they convey. Typically consisting of small jingles in a circular frame, they come with or without a drum head. Square- and triangular-shaped tambourines have appeared throughout history, across the Mediterranean region, in ancient Greece and Rome, and all the way through the Middle East.

Various types of music feature the tambourine, and it resounds in the folk music of Greece, Turkey, and Italy. Children will likewise feel the joy and pride of making and playing their own tambourines.

You will need

- 2 firm paper or plastic plates
- Hole punch
- Pencil
- Paints, stickers, and/or fabrics
- Craft glue
- Stapler
- Jingle bells (6 to 8)
- Pipe cleaners (or twist ties)
- Recordings (favorite, with or without tambourine)

1 Gather together all of the necessary items for the construction of the tambourine.

Shake that tambourine *continued*

2 Start by punching six to eight evenly spaced holes around the rim of a firm paper or plastic plate. You can help your child to do this.

3 Align the first plate over the top of a second plate, so that they are in a convex face-to-face position. Use a pencil to draw through the holes of the first plate to the second plate. Follow through by punching holes at the pencil marks of the second plate.

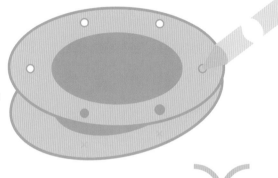

4 Help your child to decorate the outer edges of the two plates, using paints, stickers, or pieces of fabric.

5 Show your child how to string a pipe cleaner or twist tie through each of your jingle bells. Twist the ends of each tie to secure.

6 With the two decorated plates in a convex face-to-face position, thread one pipe cleaner or twist tie (with jingle bell) through each hole. Turn each tie back on itself and twist to secure in place. Your child can help you with this.

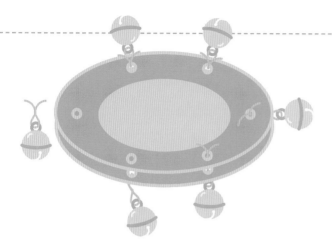

Other activities to try

Find some notable tambourine players in popular music, and look out for examples of them to listen to and view: Stevie Nicks of Fleetwood Mac, Davy Jones of The Monkees, and Mick Jagger of The Rolling Stones.

- -

Listen to examples of tambourine cousins such as the pandeiro (Portugal, Brazil) or the riq and the daf (Middle East).

7 Show your child how to shake the tambourine to make sound. Encourage her to shake it freely at first, and then to try establishing a rhythm.

8 As a second technique, show your child how patting the center of the tambourine can make the instrument jingle in a different way.

9 Play the tambourine to a selection of recordings, such as Tchaikovsky's "Trepak" from *The Nutcracker Suite*. Play a steady beat, or a repeated rhythm pattern, by tapping the tambourine or by playing freely with arms up in the air in a high shake. Show your child the different movements first, then let her try for herself.

Rise-and-shine music

There is truth to the statement that waking up is hard to do! It's sometimes challenging for your child to get up from beneath warm, cozy blankets, and at times it may take the reminder of a good breakfast, a play date, or some other activity to motivate that wake-up. While a smile and a bright voice of good cheer are productive, so, too, is music. Children respond well to the sunny sound of a singing voice, a familiar song, or a favorite recording.

You will need

- Recordings of morning music (optional)
- Music box or other wind-up music-making toy

Other activities to try

Waking up happy is helped by the sound of these popular songs: "Reveille/First Call" (the Army wake-up call), "Happy" (Pharrell), "The Circle of Life" from *The Lion King*, "Shout" (The Isley Brothers), "When the Red, Red Robin Comes Bob, Bob, Bobbin' Along" (Bing Crosby), "I Can See Clearly Now" (Jimmy Cliff), or the melody from "Morning" (Edvard Grieg). Play recordings of these pieces, or sing their melodies.

Wake-up verses

Choose one or more of these for your wake-up call, or use them as inspiration for making up your own verses.

*Rise and shine, and make a little time
For the happy day that's here for us to split and share so fine.*

*Wake up, sleepyhead, and jump into the day.
Time to be together and to play and come-what-may.*

*Alive, alive, and it feels so good.
Wake up in the morning, start the day as we should!*

*Hop right out and stretch yourself and join the brand new day,
Good morning to you: It's time for work—and play!*

1 A rise-and-shine song can be the perfect opening of a new day. Play with the possibilities of creating your very own wake-up song with your child. When putting together the lyrics, consider words, phrases, and sentiments along the following lines: Good morning; morning hugs; open up your eyes; a brand new day; *buenos días; bonjour; guten tag.*

2 See the verses (right). Speak them aloud, and find a rhythm for them. Choose one to know well, and chant it at a moderate speed, increasing the tempo with each repeated pronunciation.

3 Turn the chant into a song, allowing an easy but energetic melody to come forward. Mix and match the phrases, or vary them.

4 Sing your song often, and with energy. It will become very familiar and serve as a welcome wake-up signal for your child.

5 Choose a little music box or music-making toy to play softly in the ear of your little one. Follow that with the wake-up song you have created.

Our holiday music

The familiar seasonal songs of our holidays allow children to know that they are a part of a family; a community; and cultures with histories, values, and interests. There are songs for every holiday and for every season. Many of them are already in our ears, heard and learned from our own early childhood experiences. We need no music notation to bring these songs to life, and they may naturally be revealed (and remembered by us) in the mediated music that pours out of our TVs, radios, and online music sources, and in public spaces that we visit. Children take these songs into their own lives, too, listening up and eventually joining in as they celebrate the holidays.

1. Remember the songs of the holidays from your childhood, and how they excited you and taught you the traditions of the season.

2. Sing these holiday songs to your child—at bedtime and nap time, after meals, in the car, or on a walk.

3. Add rhythm instruments and gestures to enliven the songs and provide "verve" and spirit. Choose one of the instruments you have already made with your child—for example, a rattle or a tambourine.

4. Engage in an anthropological fieldwork project by talking with family members and friends to find out their favorite songs of the holidays.

5. Learn a new song for holidays you may be less familiar with—be it the Chinese New Year, Rosh Hashanah, Kwanzaa, Diwali, Mardi Gras, or Eid al-Fitr. Record it and listen carefully, especially in the case of songs in unfamiliar languages.

Another activity to try

Discuss why, when, and where a particular song is sung; who sings it; and whether the song includes instrumental accompaniment or dance. The history of people in a particular place or time may be wrapped into the meaning of a song.

Holiday songs

There are countless holiday songs to choose from. Yours may include:

"Auld Lang Syne" (New Year's); *"Cockles and Mussels" (St. Patrick's Day); "Here Comes Peter Cottontail" (Easter); "La Raspa" (Cinco de Mayo); "Five Little Pumpkins" (Halloween); "Over the River and Through the Woods" (Thanksgiving); "Hanukkah, Oh Hanukkah" (Hanukkah); "Jingle Bells" (Christmas)*

Songs with friends and family

Children make music alone and together, each of which can be valued for its outcomes of independent expression and collaboration. Group singing and playing is exhilarating in that the sound that begins with the individual is joined by one or more others, and the music comes back as something quite thrilling in its strength and unity. Music making in the group begins at home in the family, with siblings—and with little cousins and friends, too—and the results are gratifying and therapeutic to children. In fact, this early ensemble work may prepare children for a lifetime of positive musical and social experiences to come.

You will need

- Group of children (friends, siblings, cousins)
- Various rhythm instruments
- Pretend mic

1 Assemble two or more children together for a group music experience. Tell them that sharing is always a positive behavior, including the sharing of music for the joy of making something beautiful together.

2 Ask that each child choose a favorite song to lead. Have a set of songs ready, too, for sharing (see page 106). The song leader may use a pretend mic in sharing the song with others.

3 After noting the songs that seem most familiar, or that the children are especially fond of, lead the children in singing them together. Give a starting pitch within the range of the children's singing voices by singing it first on a phrase like "here-is-the-starting pitch." Then, acting like a conductor, raise your hands to the level of your head (signaling attention), and drop them to about your waistline as you and the children sing the very first word of the song.

Other activities to try

Make a simple pretend mic when sharing songs by covering an empty toilet paper tube with foil, scrunching a second piece of foil into a ball, and gluing this to the top of the foil-covered tube.

Combine singing and playing together, inviting children to sing one of their shared songs while also keeping the beat on their instruments and objects, and still staying in tune and in time together.

Tip Adult voices are generally lower than children's voices, so listen carefully to their natural speaking and singing voices as you set a pitch for their singing together. If the song is pitched too low, they will either not be able to sing at that range or will sing in an unnatural manner.

4 Continue to wave your hands in conducting fashion so that children do not rush the singing. Some songs will feel good in a 1-2 rhythm (hands down on 1 and up on 2), while others may move in a 1-2-3 rhythm (hands down on 1, hands out and away from the body on 2, hands up on 3) or in a 1-2-3-4 rhythm (hands down on 1, hands in and together on 2, hands out and away from the body on 3, hands up on 4).

5 Practice makes perfect: Help the children to watch and listen as they start each song together and as they stay together. Starting and stopping singing is an important ensemble technique that can be learned early on if the children are able to focus.

6 Encourage children to conduct the song themselves, supplying gestures that cue starts and stops. They might take turns "at the front" in conducting the songs.

Songs to sing

Choose one of the following songs to sing, or encourage each child to volunteer one of his or her own:

"Amazing Grace"; "Frère Jacques"; "Michael (Row the Boat Ashore)"; "Rock-a-My Soul"; "Simple Gifts"; "This Little Light of Mine."

Sounds for a story

Stories are wonderful occasions for developing a child's language skills, vocabulary, and a basic fluency of words and new phrases. By reading them aloud to a child, there comes the opportunity to turn the stories into little musical performances. Whether the stories are about music and musicians or not, vocal sounds and sounds on instruments and sound-making objects can be inserted here and there. With each telling, additional layers of sound can be added to a story, and even dramatizations of characters and their activities within the tale.

You will need

- Storybooks
- Instruments and sound-making objects

1 Choose a book to read aloud that will entice your child to imagine sounds to enhance the events in the story (see page 108 for some examples).

Sounds for a story *continued*

2 Read the story to your child with feeling and expression. Allow your voice to rise and fall with excitement, suspense, sadness, and joy. Pause to give time for the meaning of words—or to allow your child to repeat the words—and to provide an opportunity to think of sounds to go with that moment within the story.

3 Gather instruments and sound-making objects together. Include homemade instruments; bells and whistles; kitchen pots, pans, and utensils; garden tools; and various items that can be blown, drummed, and strummed. Think about vocal and body-sound potential. Sounds may be invented for points in the story plot; as signals for particular characters; and for openers, closers, and transitions in the story.

Stories to read

Here are some examples of stories that you might try:

Polar Bear, Polar Bear, What Do You Hear?
Beethoven Lives Upstairs
Crash! Bang! Boom!
Her Piano Sang: A Story about Clara Schumann
Mole Music
The Philharmonic Gets Dressed
The Singing Man: Adapted from a West African Folk Tale
Sounds All Around
Zin! Zin! Zin! A Violin!

4 Re-read the story aloud in order to integrate the music and sounds. Prepare for a presentation of the story to one or more listeners, smoothing out the timing of the insertions.

5 Turn the story into a dramatic affair by encouraging your child to act out one or more of the characters and their adventures. Add costumes (a scarf for a cape, a skirt for a long dress, and/or hats) and props, which can be helpful in delivering more of the story.

Other activities to try

Consider also the age-old stories that you know by heart and that will not require the use of a book. *Three Little Bears*, *Little Red Riding Hood*, and *Hansel and Gretel* may flow well and allow you to be more playful in your storytelling.

Use Worksheet 9 to help prepare characters for a story your child wants to dramatize.

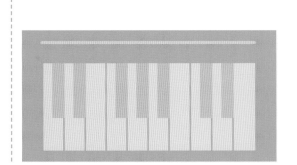

Nap-time songs and sounds

Children need restorative sleep time. Following an active morning and a healthy lunch, the rhythm of the day often drifts to quiet-time activity and a nap of an hour or two. Music and nap time help in preparing children for more complex activities and social interactions later in the day. Children need this down time in order to relax and allow some processing of the day's activity, while also restoring their energy for what's to come.

You will need

- Bedtime story books
- Recordings of soothing music
- A stuffed animal or doll

1 Ease into nap time with a pleasant and not-too-active story (see suggestions for nap-time stories, opposite).

2 A signal song may encourage resting time. It could be a lullaby or something specific to the midday nap. It may include short and repetitive verses that convey a message of repose and relaxation. Make up a nap-time song of your own.

3 Play recordings of music that moves slowly, such as "The Swan" and "Aquarium" from Saint-Saëns' *The Carnival of the Animals*, Brahms's "Waltz in A-Flat Major" (Opus 39, No. 15), Debussy's "Clair de Lune," or Chopin's "Nocturne in E-Flat Major" (Opus 9, No. 2).

4 Encourage your child to conjure up peaceful images of the day, or to imagine the movement of animals to music you might play.

5 Have your child choose a favorite stuffed animal or doll to stroke gently while listening to a story or music.

Nap-time stories

You and your child may have favorite stories of your own. Here are some others to try:

Fantastic Mr. Fox (by Roald Dahl)
Now We Are Six (by A. A. Milne)
Goodnight Moon (by Margaret Wise Brown)
If You Give a Mouse a Cookie (by Laura Numeroff)
The Rainbow Fish (by Marcus Pfister)
The Story of Ferdinand (by Munro Leaf)
Corduroy (by Don Freeman)

Tip Up to about the age of five or six years, children do well with a nap. The younger they are, the longer the nap they need. By the time a child enters into school, nap time may morph into quiet time with stories and music.

Outdoor music

Sticks and stones

As the weather allows, we open the doors for our young children to waddle, wiggle, and wander beyond walls. The open air awakens and energizes little voices and bodies and motivates their exclamations of glee. The yard invites exploration, as does the garden or park in the neighborhood. In this chapter, you will find prospects for you and your child to sing, dance, and play together in the outdoors as you make time to explore and examine the sounds of the world in which you live.

Musical sounds from rocks? From the sounds of rocks thrown into water? This is just the beginning of the possibilities for the making of music in the outdoors. Nature provides many possibilities: sticks, leaves, birds, and animals offer sounds that approximate rhythm or melody. You can seek out these sounds with your child and respond to them. Your child may be inspired by natural sounds to create new songs and instrumental pieces.

There is music to be found in cars and music to be made using garden tools. When children are swinging in the yard or a public park, or teetering on a seesaw, the movement of these rides may give way to rhythms, rhymes, chants, and songs. The very idea of being outdoors will bring a sense of elation to children, and this feeling may result in singing and dancing creatively in the outdoors.

Dancing in the open air

Creative dance in the open air, on soft grassy ground, can be completely liberating. Unless a powerful system is available to pump the sounds into the designated outdoor space, the music for outdoor dancing may be completely unamplified and acoustic. Or, there may be no externally sounding music at all, in which case the creative dance may be driven exclusively by an internalized musical rhythm sensed and shared by you and your child.

You will need

- Wide open space
- Materials that flow: scarves, ribbons, streamers

Dancing in the open air *continued*

1 Begin with some you-then-me bends and stretches, in which you and your child take turns in providing ideas for tuning up the body for dance.

2 Provide some movement ideas, again in an imitative procedure in which you lead and your child follows. Model high- and low-stepping movement in place and across space, holding arms high and wide and then low and close to the torso. Touch shoulders, chest, tummy, knees, and toes. Clap and pat.

3 Step sideways and backward, slowly at first and then picking up speed. Turn right and then left, sink low and rise high, twirl and spin. Step straight and crooked; tired and energetic; in a circle, a square, or a figure eight. Step and stomp like a giant; a mouse; and as if your feet are stepping into snow, mud puddles, or high water.

Tip
- An ideal outdoor space for dancing will consist of fairly level ground that is thickly cushioned by high-density soft grass, unobstructed by rocks and paths, and far from the traffic of city streets.
- Watch that any materials are not overly long to trip your child during use.

4 Explore moving together. Take one hand, or both hands, and step forward, sideways, and back. Turn together, separately, and back together again.

5 Standing still, listen for natural sounds that may suggest movement: the sound of running water, the wind through the trees, or bird cries and calls.

6 For one movement piece, tie scarves, long ribbons, or streamers to hands, waists, and shoulders—these may affect the quality and flow of the creative dance.

Another activity to try

If music is available, follow it as a guide to improvised free dancing. The pulse is a guide to the speed of the movement, while the dynamics and choppy or smooth style will dictate the character of the movement. Listen for repeated melodies and rhythms, which will suggest repeating a movement.

Sticking with the music

A stick is a piece of wood that has fallen from a tree—it is smaller than a branch but bigger than a twig. For children, sticks can be used to draw in the dirt, can act as pretend swords and fishing poles, or can be put to use digging up small rocks and other items from the ground. Sticks can also be brought into the musical realm, inspiring musical play.

You will need

- Sticks of assorted shapes and sizes

1 Experiment with stick sounds with your child: Tap them on different surfaces, tap them together, snap them in two, or rub two sticks together. Break a stick from a tree, listening to the cracking sound it makes. How many different ways can you think of to create a variety of sounds? Count them with your child.

2 Take turns echoing stick patterns. After you tap your stick in a pattern (such as long-long-short-short-long), invite your child to repeat it. Make the pattern longer each time to see how much your child can remember. Then, switch places so that your child creates the patterns. Don't worry if his patterns do not always seem logical—the simple act of inventing something that you try to imitate affirms his creative impulses.

3 Find some dirt and use a good-sized stick to draw a long, wavy line in the dirt. Follow the contour of the line with your voices, making higher and lower sounds as the line moves over the ground. No need to use real words here—"oooOOOooo" sounds work just as well.

4 Children love to drum. Find two sticks of roughly the same size, spanning the length from your child's elbow to his fingertips. Sit him on the ground outside, with his legs spread apart, and encourage him to drum away with the sticks. After drumming as hard as he can—likely his first instinct—see if your child can vary the loudness of the drum pattern, going from loud to soft to loud again.

Another activity to try

Sometimes, we see a conductor of Western classical music directing an orchestra by waving a baton. Invite your child to be a conductor. Line up some stuffed animals, play some music, and watch your child wave a stick around, leading his "orchestra" through the music.

Rock music

We think of rock music as the joyful music that blasts from the speakers of our cars as we drive. But real rocks can make musical sounds that are remarkably varied. Made of minerals that have hardened together over time, a rock can be as small as a grain and as large as a mountain. Musically, the varying qualities of rocks can affect the sounds that can be made using them.

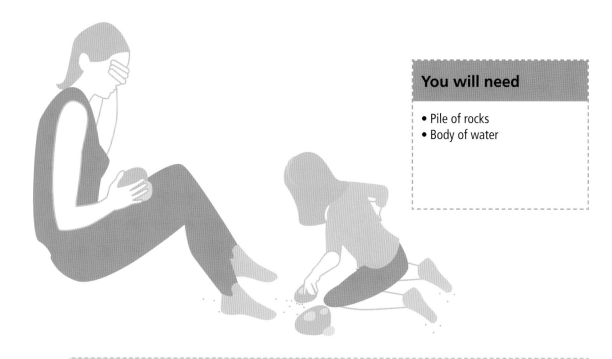

You will need

- Pile of rocks
- Body of water

Tip   Tapping rocks together is an activity that could conceivably result in hurt fingers. Help your child to hold the rock in a way that will protect those sensitive body parts.

1. Go outside with your child and find two rocks about the size of her hand. Experiment with the rocks, tapping them against different hard surfaces—a street or a stop sign, a wooden fence, a metal railing. Choose your two favorite sounds. With each of you holding one rock, make a pattern of your rock sounds.

2. Ask your child to think about what affects the sound. Take the rocks you have collected, and make a prediction: If you tap each rock on the pavement, will the sound be the same? Does the sound change if two rocks are different sizes?

3. Once you have listened for the sounds of different rocks against the pavement, take turns closing your eyes. As one of you closes your eyes, the other taps a rock against the ground. See if you can identify which rock made the sound.

4. Collect pebbles and rocks in a variety of shapes and sizes, and take them to the water. Throw the different rocks into the water, marveling at the different sounds that the rocks make. A river, lake, or ocean is ideal, but a bathtub can work just as well if you keep the rocks and pebbles on the small side.

Another activity to try

For the older child, try asking her to keep the beat, tapping two rocks together while you sing a song or listen to a piece of music.

Garden tool music

Hoes, rakes, shovels, spades, and shears—in a myriad of ways, garden tools help us beautify the land that surrounds us. Centuries ago, such tools were made of wood or even bone, but today, they are mostly made of iron and steel. The durability of these metals boosts their usefulness in our work in the garden— and also leads to some distinctive opportunities when it comes to sound exploration.

You will need

- Assortment of garden tools

1 Take garden tools of three different sizes, such as a rake, a shovel, and a trowel (the exact items aren't important, just that they are different sizes). Line them up on the ground, in order of largest to smallest. Pointing to each one, name them "high rake," "medium shovel," and "low trowel," singing the names in a higher or lower voice. Ask your child to repeat each name after you.

2 Name that instrument! Take a small garden tool such as a spade, and listen for the different sounds as you tap it against three different garden tools. Repeat a couple more times, then invite your child to close her eyes. As you tap one "instrument," see if your child can identify the instrument making the sound.

3 Memorize a garden poem (see right). Choose some favorite pairs of garden tools to accompany the poem, using them to tap along with the words. The tapping can occur on the beat, at the end of each phrase or stanza, or at anytime throughout the poem.

Garden poetry

Here is a poem by Beatrix Potter you can try. Alternatively, use a garden poem that you and your child like to recite.

We have a little garden,
A garden of our own,
And every day we water there
The seeds that we have sown.
We love our little garden,
And tend it with such care,
You will not find a faded leaf
Or blighted blossom there.

Tip Watch for sharp edges and points on your garden tools. In most cases, a paper towel can be folded and placed over any potential hazard areas.

Ode to nature

There is currently a movement to connect children and nature, and there are various ways to learn and enjoy it. Family walks in parks inspire questions about flowers, trees, bushes, insects, and animals. In all of these experiences, music may play a part as we listen for sounds, learn (and create) songs and chants about nature, and sing songs as the movement of walking and watching ripples and waves stimulates them.

You will need

- Sounds in nature
- Poems

Tip

Watch for trail conditions on hikes, and load a pack with water, snacks, and extra layers of clothing for even an hour's walk. Keep your child in constant sight of you—not too far ahead or far behind.

1. Take a hike with your child in a forest or city park, and stand silently for five minutes to listen to the sounds. Count how many sounds there are with your child, and identify their sources (the wind through the trees, birds, animals like squirrels and chipmunks, a distant river or waterfall). Play this game at different places on the hike, and compare the sounds.

2. While walking in a park, in the forest, or by water, pay attention to the rhythm of the walking movement. Sing familiar songs with your child that naturally coincide with rhythms of walking at various speeds.

3. In a forest, hunt for objects that make sound. Find sticks of various shapes and sizes for tapping rhythms on a tree trunk, and rocks for tapping against other rocks and found objects.

4. Take inspiration for music from water. Try walking along a stream, throwing pebbles, or skipping rocks on the edge of a stream or pond, renting a canoe or rowboat to paddle, going fishing, or catching frogs, and see if songs don't emerge in the playfulness: "Row, Row, Row Your Boat," "Big Boat up the River," "The Erie Canal."

Nature poetry

Here are some poems about nature that you might try, with suggestions for movement while walking.

Apples, peaches, pears, and plums,
Tell me when your birthday comes:
January, February, March...
(Recite the poem together, and stop on the month of your child's birthday).

Fishy, fishy in the brook.
Daddy catch him with a hook.
Mommy fry him in a pan,
Baby eat him like a man.
(Mime the actions of the story, and replace baby with the name of your child.)

Fuzzy Wuzzy was a bear.
Fuzzy Wuzzy had no hair.
Fuzzy Wuzzy wasn't fuzzy, was he?
(Invite your child to hold a teddy bear and stroke his fur rhythmically.)

Songs of the cuckoo

Birds are nature's musicians. Throughout history and everywhere in the world, birds have called, cried, signaled, and sung in ways that appear melodic and rhythmic to the human ear. Their music has captured the imagination of composers such as Mozart, Tchaikovsky, Vivaldi, and Messiaen, among others. The cuckoo, with its cosmopolitan presence across the world's continents, is one of the best known of birdcalls (or songs) that resemble whistles or flutes. Children's listening skills can be put to the test by focusing on the cuckoo sound that is so very distinguishable, as well as by discerning the music of other birds living nearby.

1 Listen with your child to selections from the world of Western classical music that feature musically imagined bird music: "Hens and Roosters" (from Saint-Saëns' *The Carnival of the Animals*); Vaughan Williams's "The Lark Ascending"; Vivaldi's "La Primavera" (from *The Four Seasons*); Messiaen's "The Robin"; Mozart's aria featuring Papageno and Papagena, in *The Magic Flute*; and Stravinsky's "Dance of the Firebird" (from *The Firebird Suite*).

You will need

- Selection of recordings
- Internet
- Whistles, slide whistles, and recorders

2 The cuckoo's call is favored by many people in many places over time, and its "cuc-koo" is heard in the Swiss cuckoo clocks as well as in traditional songs in England and old Anglo-American communities. Listen to the musical call of the cuckoo every quarter of an hour on a cuckoo clock, and in songs about the cuckoo, as it begins on a higher pitch and drops to a lower pitch.

3 Sing the sound of the cuckoo in imitation of the Swiss clock and its sound in various cuckoo songs. Invite your child to copy you. Point out the higher sound that is followed by the lower sound, and work together to find an instrument with which to play the sound.

4 Find examples of birdsong by listening to their sounds in the neighborhood. Seek out their sounds on the Internet, too, from blackbirds and thrushes to chickadees, robins, blue jays, and cardinals. Challenge your child to imitate the birdsong she hears.

5 With whistles, slide whistles, and recorders, listen to and imitate birdsong and bird calls.

Another activity to try

Inspired by the sounds of the cuckoo and other birds, and by the compositions of Western art music composers, work with your child to create music for whistles, slide whistles, and recorders that pays homage to her favorite birds.

Dogs, cats, and other animals

Animals delight young and old alike. Whether they be common household pets (cats, dogs, or hamsters), farm animals (cows, chickens, or pigs), or animals many of us only see in the zoo (pandas, elephants, or monkeys), we are mesmerized by the ways they look and move. Children are fascinated, too, by the wide variety of noises that animals can make, a bounty of sounds that allow us to identify what is special about being human.

1 For many young children, some of the first words they speak are the names of animals. Yet even before they speak words, many small children learn to imitate animal sounds. Review the sounds that different animals make with your child. Encourage your child to think about the highs and lows of the different sounds. For example, is a cat's meow at a higher pitch than a dog's bark? What about the difference between a kitten and a cat? Does an elephant's trumpet sound high, or low, or both?

2 Make different animal calls and ask your child which ones are higher sounds and which ones are lower. Try out sounds for a cat, dog, cow, rooster, chicken, horse, and bird—or any other animals your child knows and loves. Experiment with different ways to make the same animal sound higher and lower.

3 For children, the "head voice" is the higher part of their vocal range and has a gentler quality than their lower "chest voice." Some children discover that quality of their singing easily, while for others it takes a longer time. Animal sounds are a time-tested way for young children to attain that head voice. Get your child to meow like a small kitten, to hoot like an owl, and to squeak like a mouse—the possibilities are endless.

4 Speak a short children's poem that you and your child know. After speaking it together in a regular voice, speak it like an elephant, in a lower voice. Then, repeat the poem like a mouse might do it, in a higher voice.

5 With your child, brainstorm the different songs that he knows about animals, and sing them.

Other activities to try

If your family has a pet, make up a song about it. No need to worry about a beautiful melody or rhyming words—just create an ode to the animal that many children think is the most important member of the family.

Use Worksheet 10 to make some musical puppets.

Music in the car

Many children spend a great deal of time in the car, traveling from home to school and back, and to the variety of activities that fill our lives. The popularity of toy cars, those fist-sized playthings that youngsters zoom around the carpet, testifies to their fascination for children. The time spent traveling in a car can be a great opportunity for family time. It can also be a prime time for musical exploration.

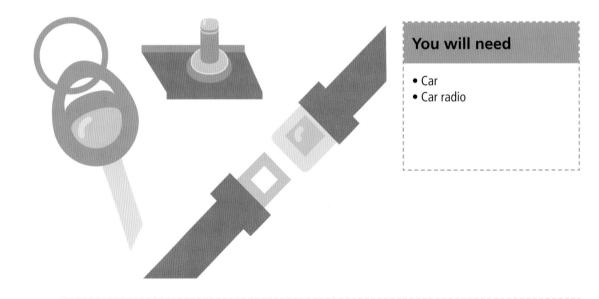

You will need

- Car
- Car radio

Tip   If your child has difficulty naming sounds, provide an example of a sound that you don't hear. For example, as you climb into the car, you could ask, "Did you hear an elephant roar?" "How about a door opening?" Providing such an example may lead your child to more easily identify the sounds around him.

1 With your child, name all the sounds that you hear as you get into the car. Go slowly, listing each sound along the way—the creak of a door opening, the thwack when the door closes, the click of the seat belt, and the jingling of the keys are just some of the sounds that you may hear as you prepare for your trip.

2 As you are driving, open the car windows. Repeat the activity in Step 1, now listening for all the different sounds you hear as the car is moving—the wheels on the pavement, the vroom of the motor, the horn of a passing car. How many different sounds can you and your child name? Ask your child to identify how they differ from what you heard when the car started. For a good laugh, encourage your child to imitate the different sounds that she hears.

3 Take a tour through the stations on the radio. Find one radio station, listen for about thirty seconds, and decide together if you like the song or not. Turn the dial to the next station, and then the next, repeating the process to discuss your preferences. Don't be afraid to disagree—it can provide your child with an opportunity to develop and articulate an independence of opinion.

Another activity to try

Do an Internet search for "Car Song," a classic piece by folksinger Woody Guthrie. Sing along with your child.

Musical seesaws and slides

Like swings, seesaws are commonly found in children's play areas. When the seesaw follows an even motion due to a balancing of equal weight on each end, there is a slow rhythm that kicks into action. Another common ride in playgrounds is the slide. These two playground rides have appealed to children's playful nature for generations and are curious launches to musical expression.

You will need

- Seesaws and slides in a public park
- Piano, keyboard, piano app

1 Take a trip with your child to a public park. Encourage her to try out the slide and the seesaw.

2 Talk about the experiences of the seesaw and the slide. Prompt feelings of the give-and-take of the seesaw's sensation of rising in the air and then falling, and the exhilaration of a speedy ride down the slide. However she describes them, these playground rides are likely sources of euphoric feeling of joy.

3 Share playground-related poems with your child (see right), reciting them aloud and in rhythm. As in all poetry, their recitation out loud and repeatedly will enable the words and syllables to fall into a regular rhythm that may suggest movement.

4 Back home, while using a piano, keyboard, or piano app, create two short yet distinctive musical pieces with your child to express the sensations of riding a seesaw and a slide. The music may (or may not) be sung and may be all or partly instrumental, but they should personify the feeling of riding each of the two playground rides.

Playground poetry

Try the following poems or select a couple of your own. Note that the second poem is structured in two parts for every line, the first of which is the main message, while the second (R, for Response) can be quickly and easily learned by your child.)

Seesaw, Marjory Daw, eevy,
* ivy, over.*
Teeter and totter and what does
* it matter?*
Up and then down, up-down-all-
* around.*
Seesaw, Marjory Daw, eevy,
* ivy, over.*

The slippery slide is a very fast
ride. **(R: Very fast, very fast, very**
fast ride)
You step up to the top with your
eyes open wide. **(R: Eyes open,**
eyes open, eyes open wide)
You sit high on your seat and
look out to the view. **(R: The view,**
the view, the beautiful view)
Then you push off the side,
screaming loud as you do:
The slippery, slippery, slippery slide

Music that swings

There is nothing like the feel of a good swinging motion—on swings in a public park or schoolyard, as well as in the rhythm of a 6/8 song that lands in a rock-solid *1* before rising up on *2*. For children, this swing rhythm—where just six beats are played in an eight-beat bar—is evident in nursery rhymes, chants, and songs, and is enjoyed as a swaying or side-to-side rocking movement.

You will need

- Swings in a public park
- Drum and sticks (or pot and spoons)

Singing activity

Sing some of these lines for the song activity in Step 5.

Here we go 'round the mulberry bush,
  the mulberry bush, the mulberry bush.
Here we go 'round the mulberry bush,
  so early in the morning.

The farmer in the dell, the farmer in the dell.
Heigh-ho, the derry-o, the farmer in the dell.

1 Take a trip together to a public park and enjoy some riding time on swings.

2 Back home, imagine swinging on swings and the feel of swinging down (on *1*) and up again (on *2*). Count "1-2-3 4-5-6" in a fast 6/8 rhythm. Sway (or rock) from side to side, moving one direction on *1* and the opposite direction on *2* (or, if you are counting fast, then the moves are on *1* and *4*).

Another activity to try

Find musical selections that feature the swinging sound. Look especially to the music of Irish jigs, some Baroque dances, baccarolles, and the Mexican *son jarocho* traditions. While listening, dance with your child in a side-by-side swaying movement.

3 Using a drum and sticks (or a pot and two spoons), play the swinging movement of 6/8. The sound will appear something like this, with sticks moving quickly and the drum sounding a slower pulse.

Sticks (spoons)	▰	▰	▰	▰	▰	▰
	1	2	3	4	5	6
Drum (pot)	●			●		

4 Sing songs with a 6/8 feeling, again swaying back and forth to feel the strong beats of *1* and *4* (or *1* and *2*, if you consider only the slower big beats). Try singing and swaying to the songs.

Music for a parade

Parades are festive occasions, and these public processions
are often meant for the celebration of a holiday or a special
event. Parades are spectacles that excite and delight children,
and parade music frequently sounds out a lively invitation to
hop, leap, and jump for joy. No parade is complete without
the marching band—a full display of costumed drummers
and dancers; decorated cars, trucks, and fire engines; and a
procession of prancing horses. Wind, brass, and percussion
instruments join in to set the pace of the core music that serves
as an engine to propel all within earshot.

You will need

- Fun assortment of musical
  instruments: children's toy
  trumpets and flutes; full-sized
  "real" rattles, sticks, and
  drums; borrowed violins
  and horns
- Found materials with musical
  potential: small branches,
  twigs, and stones; a plastic
  pail and shovel
- Friends and siblings

1 Gather the instruments with the children. Show them how to tap, toot, shake, pluck, and otherwise draw potential sounds from these instruments. Encourage the children to play them freely to explore their instrumental quality, and in a more restricted fashion that allows the sweet spot of the instrument to sound. Once a sound seems to emerge—a short rhythm on a single pitch or tone, or several pitches on a steady beat—ask each child to play it repeatedly.

2 Shift to found sounds for making the music of a parade. Stones and twigs produce interesting sounds, and the children may be curious to try different ways to click two stones or twigs together. Try other sound potentials too, such as a bicycle horn or an upside-down plastic beach pail and shovel.

3 Develop a short rhythm that can be played together, exactly the same each time, and invite the children to play it repeatedly.

4 Play in place first, and then lead the children in motion to the music, stepping forward in the shape of a circle, a box, or an imaginary line stretching from one side of the yard to the other. Leave the children to follow the shape while playing with joy, in celebration of something, or someone, or "just because."

Another activity to try

Use Worksheet 6 to introduce new rhythms to your band of musicians to play in their parade.

Resources

The worksheets that follow allow you to explore music making further with your child and reinforce the various activities of the preceding five chapters: beat, rhythm, rhyme, melody, and timbre.

Melodies: up, down, around

Signs for the sounds

Rhythms in four

Rhyming in rhythm

My favorite sing-things

Rhythms to clap, tap, and play

Color them musical

Music I can see

Hats off (and on)

Musical puppets

Worksheet 1

Melodies: up, down, around

Sing the following melodies according
to the shape of the lines. Start at the left-
hand edge of each line and follow its
path with your voice.

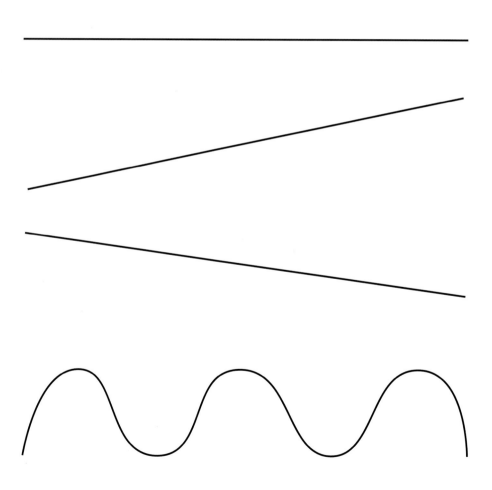

Worksheet 2

Signs for the sounds

Cut out the musical notes. With a pencil, trace their shapes
on blank paper. Color them, cut them out, and arrange them
on a bulletin board, wall, window, or other surface for a
colorful musical representation.

Rhythms in four

Cut out the four large squares and eight small round circles. Lay the squares side-by-side from left to right. Place one or two round circles in each of the four squares. The squares are the steady beat, and the circles represent claps: one "slow" clap or two "fast" claps (twice as fast as the slow clap). Clap the four-beat rhythm twice, then change the placement of the circles for a new rhythm to read and clap.

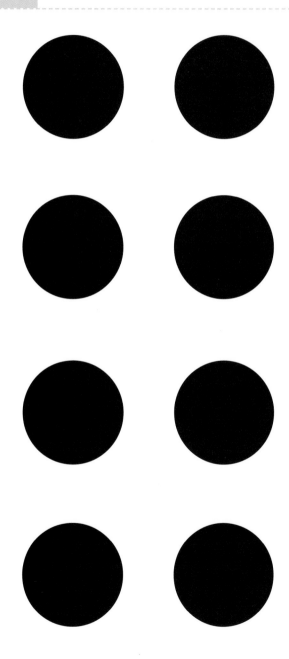

Worksheet 4

Rhyming in rhythm

Tap a steady beat and chant the rhyming words, once per beat.

Choose new words and find rhyming words for them.

Create short sentences that end with the rhyming words.

Tap the beat while chanting the rhymed sentences.

Pie:	**bye**
Hat:	**bat**
See:	**bee**
Mine:	**dine**
Hot:	**cot**
Sit:	**bit**
....	....
....	....

die	high	lie	sigh	tie	why
cat	fat	mat	pat	rat	sat
gee	he	me	she	tree	we
fine	line	mine	pine	sign	vine
dot	got	lot	pot	rot	shot
fit	hit	kit	lit	pit	wit
....	....	....	....	....	....
....	....	....	....	....	....

My favorite sing-things

What are your very favorite songs to sing?
List your top ten favorites; include only the
songs that you can sing all the way through.

1
....

2
....

3
....

4
....

5
....

6
....

7
....

8
....

9
....

10
....

Worksheet 6

Rhythms to clap, tap, and play

Starting from the left-hand side, clap, tap, or play on instruments and objects the rhythms you see here.

1

2

3

4

Color them musical

Cut out the instruments.
Color them and post them on
the refrigerator as reminders
of favorite musical sounds for
listening and playing.

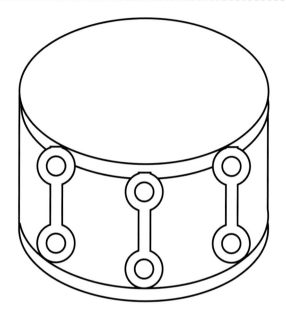

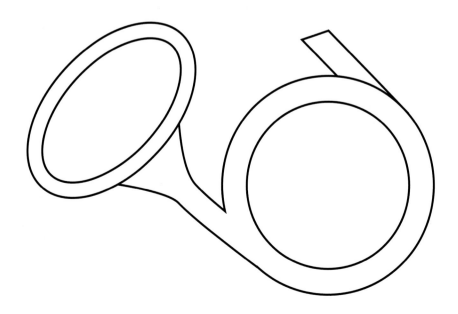

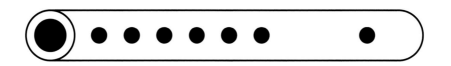

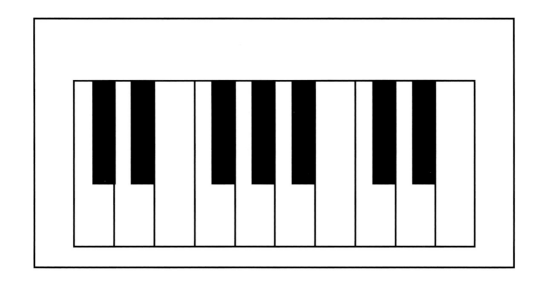

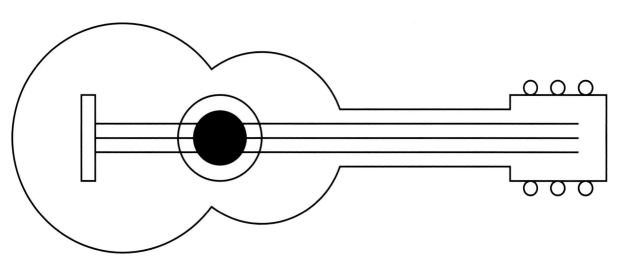

Worksheet 8

Music I can see

Listen to music that is entirely instrumental (no voices, no sung language). With crayons, draw a colorful image of what the music brings to mind. Abstract images are fine, too, with swirls, colors, and even textures that "look" like the music.

Hats off (and on)

As you sing songs that you know, think of the character you are singing about—or the character who might just be singing this song. Find materials in the house that you can wear to become that character, or make your own hat according to the sketches provided. Once you put the hat on, you can assume the role of that character and sing as he or she would sing the song.

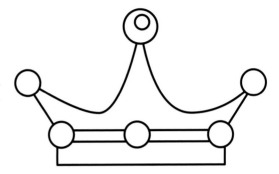

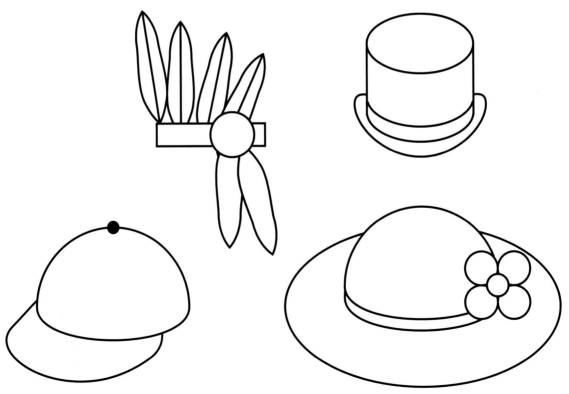

Worksheet 10

Musical puppets

Cut out the faces, color them, and glue them to small Popsicle sticks. Dance them around as you sing or listen to music.

Recordings for children

The following musical titles are a list of classical and jazz music recordings for children. Occasions for listening are evident everywhere: at meals, during play, at bath time, in the car, and going to sleep. The recordings may constitute backdrops for other activities, or can be the focus of an activity as your child responds to pulse, tempo, melody, and the tone colors of instruments and voices.

An almost infinite array of musical styles are available to share with children, particularly when opening up to the world's expressive practices—from Afghanistan to Zimbabwe! The selected recordings here are limited to Western art music and jazz (jazz titles are derived from *Jazz: The Smithsonian Anthology*).

John Adams: *Short Ride in a Fast Machine*
Louis Armstrong: "West End Blues"
J. S. Bach: *Brandenburg Concerto No. 2*
Count Basie: "One O'Clock Boogie"
Ludwig van Beethoven: *Symphony No. 5*
Benjamin Britten: *Simple Symphony*
John Coltrane: *Giant Steps*
Aaron Copland: *Appalachian Spring*
Aaron Copland: *Rodeo*
Miles Davis: "Summertime"
Claude Debussy: *Children's Corner Suite*
Duke Ellington: "Isfahan"
Stan Getz and Astrud Gilberto: "The Girl from Ipanema"
Edvard Grieg: *The Peer Gynt Suite*
Herbie Hancock: "Watermelon Man"
Gustav Holst: *The Planets*
George Frideric Handel: *Water Music*
Franz Joseph Haydn: *"Surprise" Symphony No. 94*

Scott Joplin: "Maple Leaf Rag"
Dmitri Kabalevsky: *The Comedians*
Zoltan Kodály: *Hary Janos Suite*
Machito and His Afro-Cubans: "Tanga"
Modern Jazz Quartet: *Django*
Wolfgang Amadeus Mozart: Variations on "Ah vous dirai-je, maman"
Modest Mussorgsky: *Pictures at an Exhibition*
Oscar Peterson: "Ol' Man River"
Tito Puente: "Airegin"
Nikolai Rimsky-Korsakov: "Flight of the Bumblebee"
Camille Saint-Saens: *The Carnival of the Animals*
Robert Schumann: *Album for the Young*
Igor Stravinsky: *The Firebird*
Pyotr Ilyich Tchaikovsky: *The Nutcracker*
Antonio Vivalidi: *The Four Seasons*
Weather Report: "Birdland"

Websites on music for children

A large variety of resources is available on the Internet. Selected sites are noted for following on children's musical interests, with a look into instruments and musical experiences (and music instruction) that is available electronically and live.

Amazon Kids Musical Instruments: *www.amazon.comb?node=166326011*

The Children's Music Web (Music education links for parents and teachers): *www.childrensmusic.org*

DJM Music (Musical instruments for children): *www.djmmusic.com/c-388-early-years.aspx*

Kindermusik (Classes of music for children and parents, together): *www.kindermusik.com*

Music Together (Classes of music for children and parents together): *www.musictogether.com*

The Land of Nod (Musical instruments): *www.landofnod.com/musical-instruments/toys-and-gifts/1*

For Small Hands: A Resource for Families (Real musical instruments for children): *www.forsmallhands.com/music-1/instruments-sound*

West Music (books, recordings, children's musical instruments, musical toys): *www.westmusic.com/c/kids-and-movement*

Glossary

Beat A main pulse or accent in music.

Chant A short song-like unit, usually more limited in pitch content than a song (for example, a chant may have just two identifiable pitches rather than the four, five, or more pitches of a song).

Cognitive Referring to the mental process of knowing and understanding.

Consonant A speech sound such as "b," "c," "d" (as opposed to a vowel sound of "a," "e," "i," "o," "u") that functions to stop the sound; most letters of the alphabet are consonants.

Contour Shape, such as found in the rise and fall of higher and lower pitches of a melody.

Eurythmics A system of physical movements that respond to music's rhythm as well as melody, form, texture, and expressive elements.

Groove A regular and insistent beat, especially in popular music.

Kinesthetic The quality of the physical movement of the body which, when featured in musical experiences, aids the acquisition of new knowledge.

Melody A sequence of pitches that comprise a song or theme.

Ode A lyrical poem that may sometimes be sung.

Ostinato A regularly repeated short rhythmic or melodic phrase.

Percussion Musical instruments such as sticks, drums, and bells that are played by striking (also played by shaking); body percussion is often included, too, which encompasses clapping, snapping, patting, stamping the feet.

Phoneme Distinctive short units of sound, such as a syllable.

Phrase A short musical idea, often separated by a breath.

Pitch The degree of highness or lowness of a tone; there are five separate pitches in many folk and traditional heritage songs.

Rhyme Correspondence of words with similar endings (such as "cat" and "hat").

Rhyming couplets In songs and poetry, two lines of the same length that have similar endings (such as "I like my white dog" and "We run, jump, and jog").

Rhythm Long, short, or combined long-short units of sound.

Rhythmicking Individual engagement in some manner of rhythmic behavior, such as clapping, tapping, nodding, stepping, skipping, or bouncing to a musical rhythm.

Swing A musical style that has a 6/8 rhythm, and which stimulates a back-and-forth rocking, nodding, or swaying movement.

Syllable A unit of speech having one vowel sound, with or without surrounding consonants (such as "I", "pie", and "pipe").

Tempo The speed of a rhythm, melody, song, chant, musical work.

Texture The combination of pitch and rhythm in ways that produce a single melody line, or melody with harmony, or multiple rhythms or melodies sounding at the same time.

Timbre The quality of musical sounds that are distinguishable by their source; for example, the different timbres or tone qualities of a violin, a piano, a trumpet, a flute, a xylophone, and a voice.

Tone A musical sound of a particular higher or lower pitch or quality.

Tone color Another term for timbre.

Verse A section of a poem, song, or chant, often in four lines of words and frequently with rhymed endings.

Vowel A speech sound such as "a," "e," "i," "o," "u" on which pitches can be sustained rather than stopped (the function of consonants).

Index

Picture credits

Corbis: 44 Femi Corazon.

DK Images: 80 Vanessa Davies.

Getty Images: 42 Jessie Jean; /136 Maria Teijeiro; 138 JGI/Jamie Grill.

iStock: 11 fatihhoca; /24, 117 AnaBGD; /28 mitgirl; /36 skynesher; /56 MmeEmil. /58 Kontrec; /85, 107 PeopleImages; /94 SolStock; /102 Elexa_Grey; /110 Monkey Business Images; /124 Frizzantine.

Shutterstock: 7 Igor Demchenkov; /16 FarFlungFotos; /78 Dragon Images; /104 Sergey Novikov; /112 Serhiy Kobyakov; /132 BestPhotoStudio.

Author acknowledgments

I am grateful for the ideas that have come from making music with my son Andrew and his little friends, and Kelly, Shannon, and Jimmie, and so many children with whom I have worked. I am indebted to the creative ideas of Dr. Christopher Roberts, music education consultant, colleague, and friend. Special thanks to husband Charlie for his enthusiastic collaboration in the musical parenting we have done together over the years.